SCOTT FORESMAN · ADDISON WESLEY

Mathematics

Math Diagnosis and Intervention System

Booklet F

**Place Value, Addition, and Subtraction
in Grades 4-6**

Overview of Math Diagnosis and Intervention System

The system can be used in a variety of situations:

- **During school** Use the system for intervention on prerequisite skills at the beginning of the year, the beginning of a chapter, or the beginning of a lesson. Use for intervention during the chapter when more is needed beyond the resources already provided for the lesson.

- **After-school, Saturday-school, summer-school (intersession) programs** Use the system for intervention offered in special programs. The booklets are also available as workbooks.

The system provides resources for:

- **Assessment** For each of Grades K–6, a Diagnostic Test is provided that assesses that grade. Use a test at the start of the year for entry-level assessment or anytime during the year as a summative evaluation.

- **Diagnosis** An item analysis identifies areas where intervention is needed.

- **Intervention** Booklets A–M identify specific topics and assign a number to each topic, for example, A12 or E10. For each topic, there is a page of Intervention Practice and a two-page Intervention Lesson that cover the same content taught in a lesson of the program.

- **Monitoring** The Teaching Guide provides both Individual Record Forms and Class Record Forms to monitor student progress.

PEARSON
Scott
Foresman

Editorial Offices: Glenview, Illinois • Parsippany, New Jersey • New York, New York

Sales Offices: Parsippany, New Jersey • Duluth, Georgia • Glenview, Illinois
Coppell, Texas • Ontario, California • Mesa, Arizona

ISBN: 0-328-07649-X

2 3 4 5 6 7 8 9 10 V084 12 11 10 09 08 07 06 05 04 03

Table of Contents

		Intervention Lesson Pages	Intervention Practice Pages	The same content is taught in the Scott Foresman-Addison Wesley Mathematics Program			
Booklet F				**Gr. 3**	**Gr. 4**	**Gr. 5**	**Gr. 6**
Place Value, Comparing and Ordering							
F1	Counting Sets of Coins	1	79	1-12	1-10		
F2	Making Change	3	80	1-13	1-11		
F3	Ways to Use Numbers	5	80	1-1			
F4	Understanding Three-Digit Numbers	7	82	1-2			
F5	Ways to Show Numbers	9	83	1-3			
F6	Reading and Writing Four-Digit Numbers	11	84	1-4			
F7	Extending Place-Value Concepts	13	85	1-5			
F8	Comparing and Ordering Numbers	15	86	1-7, 1-8			
F9	Rounding to the Nearest Ten and Hundred	17	87	1-10			
F10	Place Value Through Millions	19	88		1-2, 1-7		
F11	Place Value Patterns	21	89		1-3	1-5	
F12	Comparing and Ordering Numbers	23	90		1-5		
F13	Rounding Numbers	25	91		1-6		
F14	Place Value to Billions	27	92			1-1	
F15	Comparing and Ordering Numbers	29	93			1-2	
F16	Rounding Numbers	31	94			1-8	1-4
F17	Place Value and Rounding	33	95				1-1
F18	Comparing and Ordering Whole Numbers	35	96				1-3
Addition and Subtraction							
F19	Using a Chart to Add	37	97	1-9			
F20	Addition Properties	39	98	2-1			
F21	Relating Addition and Subtraction	41	99	2-2			
F22	Mental Math: Addition Strategies	43	100	2-5, 2-6			
F23	Estimating Sums	45	101	2-7			
F24	Over and Under Estimates	47	102	2-8	2-4		
F25	Mental Math: Counting On to Subtract	49	103	2-9, 2-10			
F26	Mental Math Strategies	51	104		2-1, 2-2		
F27	Adding Two-Digit Numbers	53	105	3-1			
F28	Adding Three-Digit Numbers	55	106	3-2, 3-3, 3-4			
F29	Estimating Sums and Differences	57	107	2-11	2-3		
F30	Regrouping for Subtraction	59	108	3-6, 3-7			
F31	Subtracting Three-Digit Numbers	61	109	3-8			
F32	Subtracting Three-Digit Numbers	63	110	3-9			
F33	Subtracting Across Zeros	65	111	3-10			
F34	Adding and Subtracting Money	67	112	3-12			
F35	Choosing a Computation Method	69	113	3-13	2-8		
F36	Adding Greater Numbers	71	114		2-5, 2-6	1-11	
F37	Subtracting Greater Numbers	73	115		2-7	1-11	
F38	Mental Math: Using Compatible Numbers and Compensation	75	116			1-3	
F39	Estimation Strategies	77	117			1-9	1-5

Counting Sets of Coins

Example

Count on to find the total value.

25¢   50¢   75¢   80¢    80¢

Total

Count on to find the total value.

1.

_____ _____ _____ _____ _____

Total

2.

_____ _____ _____ _____ _____

Total

Counting Sets of Coins (continued)

Do you have enough money to buy each item?
Count the money.
Circle **yes** or **no**.

3.

_____ yes no

4.

_____ yes no

5.

_____ yes no

6.

_____ yes no

Making Change

Example

Use pennies. Count up from the price.
Write how much change.

Price	You Pay	Your Change

To make change for 50¢, I count up from the
price of 48¢—49¢, 50¢. My change is 2¢.

Use pennies.
Count up from the price.
Write how much change.

	Price	You Pay	Your Change
1.	Reading is Fun! 27¢		_____ ¢
2.	36¢		_____ ¢

Making Change (continued)

Use pennies.
Count up from the price.
Write how much change.

Price	You Pay	Your Change
3. NUTS $1.47		_____ ¢
4. JUICE JUICE $1.49		_____ ¢
5. 71¢		_____ ¢

Ways to Use Numbers

Example 1

Numbers can be used to name, to count, to locate, and to measure.
Write how each number is used.

count   locate   measure   name

Example 2

Ordinal numbers show the order of people and objects.
Write the animal in each place.

First   Second   Third   Fourth

The ___dog___ is first in line.   The ___pig___ is 4th in line.

Write if the number is used to name,
to count, to locate, or to measure.

Use Example 2 for the question.

1.

2. Which animal is 3rd in line?

_____   _____

Ways to Use Numbers (continued)

Write if the number is used to name, to count, to locate, or to measure.

3.

_____

4.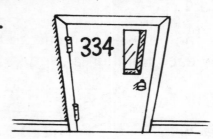

_____

Write the ordinal number that tells the place of the shape.

5.

_____

6.

_____

7. Reasoning There are 24 children waiting in line to see a movie. How many children are behind the 17th child?

_____

Test Prep Circle the correct letter for the answer.

8. How is the number used?

A locate   **B** measure   **C** count   **D** name

Understanding Three-Digit Numbers

Example

Write how many hundreds, tens, and ones.
Write the number. Read it.

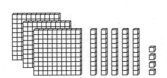

hundreds	tens	ones
3	5	4

Three hundred fifty-four _____

Write how many hundreds, tens, and ones.
Write the number. Read it.

I.

hundreds	tens	ones

_____

Understanding Three-Digit Numbers (continued)

Write how many hundreds, tens, and ones.
Write the number. Read it.

2.

_____ hundreds _____ tens _____ ones   _____

3.

_____ hundreds _____ tens _____ ones   _____

Reasoning Solve each problem.

4. Miguel has 3 bags with 100 peanuts in each bag. He also has 7 loose peanuts. How many peanuts does he have?

_____ peanuts

5. What if Miguel also has 4 small bags with 10 peanuts in each bag? How many peanuts does he have in all?

_____ peanuts

Name _____

Place-Value Patterns

Example 1

James has 162 baseball cards.
Show the number in
different ways.

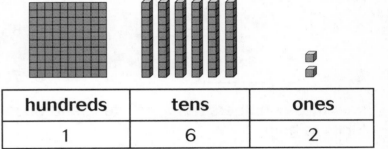

hundreds	tens	ones
1	6	2

____1____ hundred   ____6____ tens   ____2____ ones

__100__   + __60__   + __2__   Expanded Form

__162__   Standard Form   one hundred sixty-two   Word Form

Example 2

Show 162 by using just tens and ones.   1 hundred = 10 tens

1 hundred	6 tens	2 ones	Rename the hundred.
10 tens	6 tens	2 ones	Add the tens.
	16 tens	2 ones	

Write each number in standard form.

1. 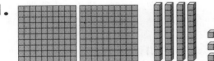   _____

2. 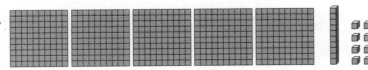   _____

Place-Value Patterns (continued)

Write each number in expanded form.

3. 462 _____ **4.** 853 _____

5. 321 _____ **6.** 760 _____

Show these numbers using only tens and ones. You may use place-value blocks to help.

7. 427 _____ **8.** 933 _____

9. 106 _____ **10.** 514 _____

Write each number in standard form.

11. six hundred twenty-two **12.** eight hundred ten

_____ _____

13. Mental Math If you rename hundreds as tens, how many tens are in 243?

_____

14. If you rename hundreds as tens, how many tens are in 782?

_____

Test Prep Circle the correct letter for the answer.

15. What is the standard form of 400 + 30 + 5?

A 4,305 **B** 405 **C** 435 **D** 430

16. If you rename hundreds as tens, how many tens are in 613?

A 61 **B** 13 **C** 6 **D** 1

Reading and Writing Four-Digit Numbers

Example 1

Use the place value chart to find the value of each digit of the
number 5,392.

thousands	hundreds	tens	ones
5	3	9	2

The 5 is in the thousands place, so the value of the 5 is
5 thousand, or 5,000.

The 3 is in the hundreds place, so the value of the 3 is
3 hundred, or 300.

The 9 is in the tens place, so the value of the 9 is 9 tens, or 90.

The 2 is in the ones place, so the value of the 2 is 2 ones, or 2.

Example 2

Write the number 5,392 in expanded form.

Use the value you found for each digit in Example 1. Then write
the number as the sum of the values.

So, the expanded form of 5,392 is: 5,000 + 300 + 90 + 2.

Write each number in standard form.

1. 1,000 + 500 + 20 + 7   **2.** nine thousand, four hundred

_____   _____

3. 8,000 + 100 + 30   **4.** five thousand, six hundred one

_____   _____

5. 4,000 + 500 + 2   **6.** six thousand, eight hundred ninety

_____   _____

Reading and Writing Four-Digit Numbers (continued)

Write each number in expanded form.

7. 3,716

8. 2,091

_____

Write the value of the underlined digit.

9. 1,8<u>6</u>3

10. <u>9</u>,504

11. 5,12<u>9</u>

12. <u>1</u>83

_____   _____   _____   _____

13. <u>8</u>,904

14. 2,0<u>2</u>3

15. 7,85<u>0</u>

16. 3,<u>5</u>48

_____   _____   _____   _____

17. Write the word name for 3,995.

_____

18. Write the word name for 4,716.

_____

19. Use the digits 1, 5, 7, and 3. Write the greatest possible
four-digit number using each of the digits only once.   _____

20. A small library has 3,798 books. How many thousands
of books does the library have?   _____

21. Algebra What missing number would make the number
sentence 5,000 + 800 + ■ + 6 = 5,826 true?   _____

Test Prep Circle the correct letter for the answer.

22. Which of the following is the correct standard form for the
number six thousand, eight hundred five?

   A 6,805   **B** 6,850   **C** 685   **D** 6,580

23. Which of the following is the correct value of the underlined
digit in the number 3,<u>9</u>41?

   A 9,000   **B** 900   **C** 90   **D** 9

Name _____

Extending Place-Value Concepts

Example 1

Use the place value chart to find the value of each digit of the number 382,145.

hundred thousands	ten thousands	thousands	hundreds	tens	ones
3	8	2	1	4	5

The 3 is in the hundred thousands place, so its value is 300,000.

The 8 is in the ten thousands place, so its value is 80,000.

The 2 is in the thousands place, so its value is 2,000.

The 1 is in the hundreds place, so its value is 100.

The 4 is in the tens place, so its value is 40.

The 5 is in the ones place, so its value is 5.

Example 2

Write 850,492 in expanded form.

First, find the value of each digit, then write 850,492 as the sum of the values.

So, the expanded form of 850,492 is
800,000 + 50,000 + 400 + 90 + 2.

Write the value of the underlined digit.

1. 50<u>7</u>,691   **2.** <u>9</u>25,481   **3.** <u>7</u>2,065   **4.** 118,<u>9</u>41

_____   _____   _____   _____

5. 657,10<u>4</u>   **6.** 298,1<u>6</u>3   **7.** 301,<u>1</u>215   **8.** 4<u>00</u>,900

_____   _____   _____   _____

Name _____

Math Diagnosis and
Intervention System

Intervention Lesson **F7**

Extending Place-Value Concepts (continued)

Write each number in expanded form.

9. 12,817

_____

10. 680,127

_____

11. Algebra What missing number would make the number
sentence 519,082 = ■ + 10,000 + 9,000 + 80 + 2 true? _____

12. Complete the pattern.
295,000; 294,000; 293,000; ■; ■; ■

_____

13. An internet website had 545,300 visitors in one day.
If they have 100,000 additional visitors the next day,
how many visitors did they have? _____

14. A brick manufacturer has 943,800 bricks in a warehouse.
They brought in an additional 10,000 bricks. How many
did they have in all? _____

Test Prep Circle the correct letter for the answer.

15. Which of the following is the correct value of the underlined
digit of the number 2<u>6</u>3,471?

A 600,000 **B** 60,000 **C** 6,000 **D** 600

16. Which of the following is the correct expanded form for
375,020?

A 300,000 + 70,000 + 5,000 + 20

B 30,000 + 7,000 + 500 + 20

C 300,000 + 7,000 + 500 + 20

D 300,000 + 70,000 + 500 + 20

© Pearson Education, Inc.

Comparing and Ordering Numbers

Example

Order these numbers from **least** to **greatest.**

2,457   2,491   1,245

Write the numbers with the ones digits lined up. Then compare the numbers digit by digit starting with the greatest place value.

Compare the thousands.

2,457   Since 1 thousand is less than 2 thousands, 1,245 is
2,491   the least number.
1,245

Compare the hundreds of the two other numbers.

2,457   The hundreds digits are the same, so we will
             compare the tens digits.
2,491   5 tens is less than 9 tens, so 2,491 is the greatest
             number.

The order of the numbers from **least** to **greatest** is:

1,245   2,457   2,491

Compare. Write >, <, or =.

1. 514 ◯ 512   **2.** 394 ◯ 349   **3.** 809 ◯ 809

4. 1,078 ◯ 178   **5.** 236 ◯ 2,036   **6.** 7,530 ◯ 7,240

7. 9,089 ◯ 9,098   **8.** 4,517 ◯ 5,417   **9.** 3,728 ◯ 3,727

Write the numbers in order from **least** to **greatest.**

10. 428   418   422   **11.** 1,234   134   123

_____   _____

Comparing and Ordering Numbers (continued)

Compare. Write >, <, or =.

12. 294 ◯ 2,094   **13.** 405 ◯ 450   **14.** 1,021 ◯ 1,012

Write the numbers in order from **least** to **greatest**.

15. 5,619 5,691 569   **16.** 1,010 1,001 1,100

_____   _____

17. Reasoning What is the largest digit that makes
3,465 < 3,4■5 true?   _____

18. Reasoning What is the smallest digit that makes
1,328 > 1,■28 true?   _____

19. Bob has 1,241 trading cards. Mark has 1,099 trading
cards. Who has more cards?   _____

20. Maria made 3,950 points playing a video game. Leigh
made 3,590 points. Kathy made 3,905. Order their
scores from least to greatest.

_____

Test Prep Circle the correct letter for the answer.

21. Which of the following makes the number statement
2,457 ● 2,547 true?

A >   **B** <   **C** =   **D** +

22. Missouri became a state in 1821, while California became a
state in 1850, and Pennsylvania became a state in 1787.
Which of the following shows the correct ordering of these
dates, from earliest to latest?

A 1787, 1850, 1821   **C** 1787, 1821, 1850

B 1850, 1821, 1787   **D** 1850, 1787, 1821

Name _____

Rounding to the Nearest Ten and Hundred

Example 1

Round 43, 45, and 48 to the nearest ten.

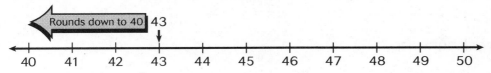

43 is closer to 40 than to 50. 43 rounds down to 40.

45 is halfway between 40 and 50. If a number is halfway between 2 tens, you round up. 45 rounds up to 50.

48 is closer to 50 than to 40. 48 rounds up to 50.

Example 2

Round 839 to the nearest hundred.

The hundreds digit is 8.

Look at the digit to the right of the hundreds place.   8<u>3</u>9

Since 3 is less than 5, round down. 839 rounds to 800.

Round to the nearest ten.

1. 68   **2.** 14   **3.** 21   **4.** 35

_____   _____   _____   _____

5. 91   **6.** 86   **7.** 47   **8.** 52

_____   _____   _____   _____

Round to the nearest hundred.

9. 761   **10.** 125   **11.** 910   **12.** 559

_____   _____   _____   _____

13. 609   **14.** 583   **15.** 445   **16.** 850

_____   _____   _____   _____

Rounding to the Nearest Ten and Hundred (continued)

Round to the nearest ten.

17. 54   **18.** 37   **19.** 81   **20.** 65

_____   _____   _____   _____

Round to the nearest hundred.

21. 609   **22.** 351   **23.** 491   **24.** 850

_____   _____   _____   _____

25. Writing in Math Round 549 to the nearest hundred and round 551 to the nearest hundred. Do you get the same answers? Explain.

_____

_____

_____

26. A rancher has 43 cattle in his herd. To the nearest ten, how many cattle are in his herd? _____

27. A new computer costs $876. To the nearest hundred, how many dollars does it cost? _____

28. Rachel has 65 coins in her coin collection. To the nearest ten, how many coins does she have? _____

29. Round 98 to the nearest ten. _____

Test Prep Circle the correct letter for the answer.

30. Which of the following is 79 rounded to the nearest ten?

   A 79   **B** 70   **C** 80   **D** 90

31. Clint has 384 baseball cards. To the nearest hundred, how many baseball cards does he have?

   A 300   **B** 400   **C** 800   **D** 80

Name _____

Place Value Through Millions

Example 1

Write 705,637,023 in word form and in short word form.

Word form: seven hundred five million, six hundred thirty-seven thousand, twenty-three in standard form; Short word form: 705 million, 637 thousand, 23

Example 2

Write the value of the underlined digit in 3<u>6</u>,925,048. The underlined digit is in the millions place, so the value of the underlined digit is 6,000,000.

Example 3

Write 21,304,201 in expanded form.

Expanded form: 20,000,000 + 1,000,000 + 300,000 + 4,000 + 200 + 1

Write each number in word form and in short word form.

1. 2,160,500 _____

_____

_____

2. 91,207,040 _____

_____

_____

3. 510,200,450 _____

_____

_____

Place Value Through Millions (continued)

Write the value of the underlined digit.

4. 4,5<u>6</u>2,398

5. 1<u>5</u>,347,025

6. 37,81<u>4</u>,956

_____   _____   _____

7. <u>5</u>26,878,953

8. 782,354,0<u>6</u>5

9. 9<u>1</u>8,403,760

_____   _____   _____

10. An underground rail system in Osaka, Japan carries 988,600,000 passengers per year. Write this number in expanded form.

_____

11. Algebra What missing number would make the number sentence 3,589,000 = 3,000,000 + ■ + 80,000 + 9,000 true?

_____

12. Math Reasoning What number can be added to 999,990 to make 1,000,000?

_____

Test Prep Circle the correct letter for the answer.

13. Which of the following gives the value of the underlined digit in the number <u>5</u>2,685,941?

A 5,000,000 **B** 50,000 **C** 500,000 **D** 50,000,000

14. The United States has about 147,200,000 car owners. Which of the following shows this number in expanded form?

A 100,000 + 40,000 + 7,000 + 200

B 100,000,000 + 40,000,000 + 7,000,000 + 200,000

C 100,000,000 + 40,000,000 + 7,000 + 200

D 10,000,000 + 4,000,000 + 700,000 + 200

Source: Factastic Book of 1001 Lists, Russell Ash, DK Publishing, 1999, pages 75, 71, and 67 respectively.

Name _____

Place Value Patterns

By using place-value you can name the same number in different ways.

10 ones = 1 ten
100 ones = 10 tens = 1 hundred
1,000 ones = 100 tens = 10 hundreds = 1 thousand

Example 1

Name 4,200 in different ways using words for place value names.

Thousands	Hundreds	Tens	Ones
4	2	0	0

42 hundreds

Thousands	Hundreds	Tens	Ones
4	2	0	0

420 tens

Thousands	Hundreds	Tens	Ones
4	2	0	0

4,200 ones

Example 2

Write 30,000 in using both words and numbers for place value names.

30,000 $\longrightarrow$ 3 ten thousands   or $3 \times 10,000$
30,000 $\longrightarrow$ 30 thousands   or $30 \times 1,000$
30,000 $\longrightarrow$ 300 hundreds   or 300×100
30,000 $\longrightarrow$ 3,000 tens   or $3,000 \times 10$
30,000 $\longrightarrow$ 30,000 ones   or $30,000 \times 1$

Name each number in two different ways using words for
place value names.

1. 900

2. 840

3. 1,600

_____   _____   _____

4. 72,000

5. 3,200

6. 14,000

_____   _____   _____

Place-Value Patterns (continued)

Name each number in two different ways using words or
numbers for place value names.

7. 700

8. 820

9. 1,200

_____

_____

_____

_____

_____

_____

10. 16,000

11. 300

12. 570

_____

_____

_____

_____

_____

_____

13. 1,400

14. 76,000

15. 8,900

_____

_____

_____

_____

_____

_____

16. The state fair ordered 2,200 new cages for the rabbit barn.
How many stacks would there be if there were 100 cages
in a stack?   _____

17. The school cafeteria has 900 lunch trays. How many
stacks of trays would there be if they were stacked 10
to a stack?   _____

18. Writing in Math What is the next number in this pattern?

2,377   2,477   2,577   _____

Explain how you know.

_____

_____

Test Prep   Circle the correct letter for the answer.

19. How many tens are in 400?

A 4   **B** 40   **C** 400   **D** 20

© Pearson Education, Inc.

Comparing and Ordering Numbers

Example

Order these numbers from **least** to **greatest**.

    2,457   2,491   1,245

Write the numbers with the ones digits lined up. Then compare the numbers digit by digit starting with the greatest place value.

Compare the thousands.

2,457   Since 1 thousands is less than 2 thousands, 1,245 is
2,491   the least number.
1,245

Compare the hundreds of the two other numbers.

2,457   The hundreds digits are the same, so we will
           compare the tens digits.
2,491   5 tens is less than 9 tens, so 2,491 is the greatest
           number.

The order of the numbers from **least** to **greatest** is:

    1,245   2,457   2,491

Compare. Write >, <, or =.

1. 514 $\bigcirc$ 512   **2.** 394 $\bigcirc$ 349   **3.** 809 $\bigcirc$ 809

4. 1,078 $\bigcirc$ 178   **5.** 236 $\bigcirc$ 2,036   **6.** 7,530 $\bigcirc$ 7,240

7. 9,089 $\bigcirc$ 9,098   **8.** 4,517 $\bigcirc$ 5,417   **9.** 3,728 $\bigcirc$ 3,727

Write the numbers in order from **least** to **greatest**.

10. 428 418 422   **11.** 1,234 134 123

_____   _____

Comparing and Ordering Numbers (continued)

Compare. Write >, <, or =.

12. 294 ◯ 2,094   **13.** 405 ◯ 450   **14.** 1,021 ◯ 1,012

Write the numbers in order from **least** to **greatest**.

15. 5,619   5,691   569   **16.** 1,010   1,001   1,100

_____   _____

17. Math Reasoning What is the largest digit that makes
3,465 < 3,4■5 true?   _____

18. Math Reasoning What is the smallest digit that makes
1,328 > 1,■28 true?   _____

19. Bob has 1,241 trading cards. Mark has 1,099 trading
cards. Who has more cards?   _____

20. Maria made 3,950 points playing a video game. Leigh
made 3,590 points. Kathy made 3,905. Order their
scores from least to greatest.

_____

Test Prep Circle the correct letter for the answer.

21. Which of the following makes the number statement
2,457 ● 2,547 true?

A >   **B** <   **C** =   **D** +

22. Missouri became a state in 1821, while California became a
state in 1850, and Pennsylvania became a state in 1787.
Which of the following shows the correct ordering of these
dates, from earliest to latest?

A 1787, 1850, 1821   **C** 1787, 1821, 1850
B 1850, 1821, 1787   **D** 1850, 1787, 1821

Rounding Numbers

Example 1

Round 79,485,360 to the nearest hundred thousand.

Step 1 Find the
hundred thousands
place.
79,4̲85,360

Step 2 Look at the digit
to the right.
↓
79,4̲85,360

Step 3 If the digit to the
right is less than 5, round
down. If the digit is 5 or
greater, round up.

Since 8 > 5, increase
the hundred thousands
place by 1.

79,485,360 rounds to 79,500,000

Example 2

Round 341,71̲8,300 to the underlined place.

Step 1 The underlined
digit is in the thousands
place.
341,71̲8,300

Step 2 Look at the digit
to the right.
↓
341,71̲8,300

Step 3 If the digit to the
right is less than 5, round
down. If the digit is 5 or
greater, round up.

Since 3 < 5, keep the
thousands place the same.

341,718,300 rounds to 341,718,000

Round each number to the nearest ten, hundred, thousand, ten thousand, and
hundred thousand.

1. 537,681

2. 1,581,267

3. 4,075,418

_____

_____

_____

_____

_____

Rounding Numbers (continued)

Round each number to the nearest ten.

4. 94,519 _____

5. 3,194,764 _____

Round each number to the nearest hundred.

6. 968,458 _____

7. 1,265,906 _____

Round each number to the nearest thousand.

8. 318,512 _____

9. 26,906,294 _____

Round each number to the nearest ten thousand.

10. 7,514,600 _____

11. 82,437,894 _____

Round each number to the nearest hundred thousand.

12. 21,561,300 _____

13. 485,629,800 _____

Round each number to the underlined place.

14. 12<u>5</u>,495

15. 7,5<u>3</u>9,461

16. 42,561,<u>7</u>35

_____ _____ _____

17. China has 124,212,400 children in primary school.
To the nearest hundred thousand, how many
children is this? _____

Test Prep Circle the correct letter for the answer.

18. Round 42,547,816 to the nearest ten thousand.

   A 42,540,000   **C** 42,500,000

   B 42,548,000   **D** 42,550,000

19. The earth is 12,756 kilometers in diameter across the equator. Round this
number to the nearest hundred.

   A 12,700   **B** 12,800   **C** 12,760   **D** 13,000

Name _____

Place Value Through Billions

Example 1

Find the value of the underlined digit in 63<u>7</u>,847,295,000.

The 7 is in the billions place.

The value of the underlined 7 in 63<u>7</u>,847,295,000 is 7,000,000,000.

Example 2

Write 637,847,295,000 in expanded form. Find the value of each digit according to its place. Then express 637,847,295,000 as the sum of the value of its digits.

The expanded form of 637,847,295,000 is: 600,000,000,000 + 30,000,000,000 + 7,000,000,000 + 800,000,000 + 40,000,000 + 7,000,000 + 200,000 + 90,000 + 5,000

Write the value of each underlined digit.

1. <u>3</u>4,906,483,201

2. <u>6</u>43,514,008,311

_____

3. 90<u>9</u>,008,446,000

4. <u>7</u>,000,574,300

_____

5. 1<u>0</u>9,321,600,004

6. <u>5</u>76,333,741,612

_____

7. Write 13,497,808,070 in expanded form.

_____

_____

8. Write 684,713,004,364 in expanded form.

_____

Name _____

Place Value Through Billions (continued)

Write the value of the underlined digit.

9. 6̲5,907,007,250

_____

10. 1̲60,379,450,000

_____

11. 43̲,614,490,712

_____

12. 6̲0,897,470,000

_____

13. The 1999 estimated population of India was
1,000,848,550. What digit is in the billions place? _____

Use the table at the right for Exercises 14–17.

14. Find the 1970 population estimate.
What is the value of the three?

_____

15. Write the 2000 population estimate in
expanded form.

World Population Estimates	
1960	3,039,332,401
1970	3,707,610,112
1980	4,456,705,217
1990	5,283,757,267
2000	6,823,766,067

_____

_____

16. How many billions lived on Earth in 1990? _____

17. How many more billions lived on Earth in 1990 than in 1960? _____

18. The 1999 estimated population for China was 1,246,871,900.
Write this in expanded form.

_____

_____

Test Prep Circle the correct letter for the answer.

19. What digit is in the ten billions place in the number six hundred
fifty-three billion, nine hundred million?

A 6 **B** 3 **C** 9 **D** 5

20. What is the value of the underlined digit? 314̲,478,494,016

A 4,000,000,000 **B** 400,000,000 **C** 4,000 **D** 40,000,000,000

Comparing and Ordering Numbers

Example

Compare 15,685,200 and 15,676,200.

Step 1 Line up the numbers
to compare the digits.

```
1 5 , 6 8 5 , 2 0 0
1 5 , 6 7 6 , 2 0 0
```
↑   ↑
same different

The ten thousands digits
are different.

Step 2 Compare the
ten thousands.

8 is more than 7, so
15,685,200 is more than
15,676,200.
You can write
15,685,200 > 15,676,200
or 15,676,200 < 15,685,200.

Compare. Use > or < for each ●.

1. 365,485 ● 343,900

2. 5,681,400 ● 5,980,100

3. 7,410,910 ● 7,412,000

4. 12,085,900 ● 12,079,900

5. 29,000,700 ● 29,000,701

6. 243,150,000 ● 243,740,000

7. 918,456,661 ● 918,423,701

8. 405,744,581 ● 405,744,568

Order the numbers from greatest to least.

9. 518,681; 51,995; 5,094,156; 5,814

_____

10. 8,205,319; 8,371,000; 80,570,000; 8,201,415

_____

11. 21,879,400; 218,794,000; 21,870,500; 2,999,900

_____

12. 975,041,700; 970,590,800; 97,900,599; 985,000,000

_____

Comparing and Ordering Numbers (continued)

Compare. Use > or < for each ●.

13. 1,689,000 ● 1,679,000

14. 43,914,500 ● 43,925,000

15. 62,441,300 ● 62,329,500

16. 518,495,000 ● 517,954,000

Order the numbers from greatest to least.

17. 96,500; 8,400,509; 8,946,000; 81,000,900

_____

18. 746,589,415; 497,956,881; 749,300,000; 719,995,800

_____

Use the table at the right for Exercises 19–21.

19. Which country is largest in population?

_____

20. Which country is least populated?

_____

21. Which country has the greater population, Peru or Venezuela?

_____

Populations	
Argentina	36,202,000
Bolivia	7,680,000
Brazil	169,545,000
Chile	14,996,000
Colombia	39,172,000
Peru	26,198,000
Venezuela	23,596,000
Note: Source: Factastic Book of 1001 Lists	

Test Prep Circle the correct letter for the answer.

22. Which number is greatest?

A 59,814,000

C 5,999,900

B 59,819,000

D 500,000,000

23. Which of these four countries has the smallest area? Brazil, 3,286,472 square miles; Canada, 3,851,788 square miles; China, 3,704,426 square miles; U.S., 3,617,827 square miles

A Brazil   **B** Canada   **C** China   **D** U.S.

Name _____

Rounding Numbers

Example 1

Round 4,142,345 to the nearest hundred thousand.

Step 1 Find the hundred thousands place.   4,1̲42,345

Step 2 Look at the digit to the right of the hundred thousands place.
If the digit to the right is less than 5, the hundred thousands digit
will stay the same. Otherwise, round up by 1.

4,1̲42,345   4 < 5, so 1 stays the same.

Step 3 Write the number, changing all digits to the right of the hundred
thousands place to zero.   4,100,000

4,142,345 rounds to 4,100,000 to the nearest hundred thousand.

Example 2

Round 6,547,024 to the nearest ten thousand.

Step 1 Find the ten thousands place 6,54̲7,024

Step 2 Look at the digit to the right of the ten thousands place.
If the digit to the right is less than 5, the ten thousands digit
will stay the same. Otherwise, round up by 1.

6,54̲7,024   7 > 5, so round 4 up to 5.

Step 3 Write the number, changing all digits to the right of the ten thousands
place to zero.   6,550,000

6,574,024 rounds to 6,550,000 to the nearest ten thousand.

Round each number to the underlined place.

1. 28,65̲4   **2.** 7̲05,418   **3.** 4,1̲73,145   **4.** 65̲,784

_____   _____   _____   _____

5. 36̲,497   **6.** 9̲21,156   **7.** 5,3̲32,487   **8.** 2̲62,147

_____   _____   _____   _____

Rounding Numbers (continued)

Round each number to the underlined place.

9. <u>8</u>,125   **10.** 2<u>9</u>5,431   **11.** <u>9</u>,333,215   **12.** 7,<u>8</u>00,473,303

_____   _____   _____   _____

13. 2<u>1</u>,236   **14.** <u>8</u>54   **15.** 98,<u>3</u>26   **16.** 985,<u>4</u>95,300

_____   _____   _____   _____

Use the information in the table for Questions 17–18.

Real Estate Sale	Amount in Dollars
Price of House	169,256
Advertising Fee	7,177
Repairs	5,873

17. What is the price of the house rounded to the nearest hundred thousand?

_____

18. What was the cost of repairs rounded to the nearest thousand?

_____

19. The Nile River, with a length of 4,180 miles, is the longest river in the world. Round the length to the nearest thousand miles.

_____

20. The Statue of Liberty is 152 feet high. What is its height rounded to the nearest ten feet?

_____

21. Number Sense   Write three numbers that would round to 44,000 when rounded to the nearest thousand.

_____

Test Prep   Circle the correct letter for the answer.

22. Round to the underlined position.   62<u>1</u>,700,000

   A 622,000,000   **B** 620,000,000   **C** 621,000,000   **D** 621,700,000

23. What is 333,456 rounded to the nearest ten thousand?

   A 333,000   **B** 334,000   **C** 330,000   **D** 300,000

Name _____

Place Value

Example

Write the number 34 billion, 115 million, 46 thousand in standard form.

Trillions			Billions			Millions			Thousands			Ones		
Hundred Trillions	Ten Trillions	Trillions	Hundred Billions	Ten Billions	Billions	Hundred Millions	Ten Millions	Millions	Hundred Thousands	Ten Thousands	Thousands	Hundreds	Tens	Ones
				3	4,	1	1	5,	0	4	6,	0	0	0

Step 1
Locate the billions period.
Write the digits starting in the
ten-billions place.

Step 2
Write in the millions places.

Step 3
Write in the thousands places
(start at the ten-thousands place).

Step 4
There is nothing in the ones places,
so write zeros in the ones places.

Standard form: 34,115,046,000
Note that the 5 in this number is in the millions place. Its value is 5 million.

Write the place and value for each underlined digit.

1. 28,6<u>5</u>4

_____

_____

2. 7<u>2</u>5,418

_____

_____

3. 4,<u>1</u>73,145

_____

_____

4. 65,<u>7</u>84

_____

_____

5. 3<u>6</u>0,049,728

_____

_____

6. <u>9</u>21,156,349,009

_____

_____

Place Value (continued)

Write each number in standard form.

7. One thousand, two hundred fifteen

_____

8. 83 million, 14 thousand, 12

_____

9. 22 trillion, 32 million, 8 thousand

_____

10. 435 million, 112 thousand, 8

_____

11. Eighty-four thousand, six

_____

12. 86 billion, 113 million, 4 thousand

_____

13. 10 trillion, 8 billion, 4 million, 4

_____

14. Ninety-six thousand, nineteen

_____

15. A college library has 10 million, 220 thousand, 312 books.
Write this number in standard form. _____

16. One country has a population of ten million, three hundred
forty-eight thousand, nine hundred forty. Write this number
in standard form. _____

17. **Number Sense** How is a zero used as a placeholder to
tell the difference between the numbers 80,321 and 8,321?

_____

_____

Test Prep Circle the correct letter for the answer.

18. Which is the place of the underlined digit?   12<u>1</u>,125,654
   A hundred thousands   **C** ten millions
   B millions   **D** hundred millions

19. Which is 34 million, 22 thousand, 316?
   A 34,000,220,316   **C** 34,220,316
   B 340,220,216   **D** 34,022,316

Comparing and Ordering Whole Numbers

Example 1

Compare two numbers by finding which number is larger.

Use > for "is greater than" and < for "is less than."

Which number is larger, 16,324 or 16,834?

Step 1: Compare the first digits on the left.
16,324　　16,834
They are the same.

Step 2: Compare the next digits.
16,324　　16,834
They are the same.

Step 3: Continue comparing digits until two digits are different.
16,324　　16,834
3 < 8

So 16,324 < 16,834.

Example 2

Order 15,271; 15,108; 14,924; and 15,203 from least to greatest.

Compare ten thousands.
They are the same.

Compare thousands.
14,924 is the least.
14,924; 15,271; 15,108; 15,203

Compare hundreds in the remaining numbers.
15,108 is the least.
14,924; 15,108; 15,271; 15,203

Compare tens in the remaining numbers.
15,203 is the least.

The numbers ordered from least to greatest are
14,924; 15,108; 15,203; 15,271

Use < or > to compare.

1. 1,467 ____ 1,465　　**2.** 78,458 ____ 78,930　　**3.** 789,037 ____ 773,409

4. 10,147 ____ 11,147　　**5.** 12,123 ____ 12,125　　**6.** 621,147 ____ 622,471

Comparing and Ordering Whole Numbers (continued)

Use < or > to compare.

7. 8,112 ____ 8,221   **8.** 418,412 ____ 481,930   **9.** 321,159 ____ 312,147

10. 20,657 ____ 21,687 **11.** 118,111 ____ 118,147 **12.** 914,146 ____ 904,168

Order the numbers from least to greatest.

13. 8,200; 820; 7,980

14. 12,984; 12,875; 11,987

15. 200; 12,945; 2,309

16. 321,984; 345,879; 323,490

17. 5,213,234; 5,123,435; 4,123,333

18. 8,740,009; 8,432,998; 8,741,234

19. Writing in Math When comparing 17,834 and 17,934, can you start by comparing hundreds? Explain.

_____

_____

Test Prep Circle the correct letter for each answer.

21. Which statement is true?

A 23,435 > 23,980   **C** 18,674 > 18,690

B 45,784 < 45,680   **D** 67,980 < 67,987

22. Which set of numbers is in order from least to greatest?

A 1,120; 11,320; 10,120

B 10,120; 11,320; 1,120

C 11,320; 10,120; 1,120

D 1,120; 10,120; 11,320

Number Patterns

Example 1

Use a hundred chart to find a pattern.

Find the pattern.

1, 5, 9, 13, ■, ■, ■
Each number is 4 more than the
number before it. Move 4 columns to
the right of each number to continue
the pattern.

$13 + 4 = 17$
$17 + 4 = 21$
$21 + 4 = 25$

So, 1, 5, 9, 13, <u>17</u>, <u>21</u>, <u>25</u>

①	2	3	4	⑤	6	7	8	⑨	10
11	12	⑬	14	15	16	17	18	19	20
21	22	23	24	25	26	27	28	29	30
31	32	33	34	35	36	37	38	39	40
41	42	43	44	45	46	47	48	49	50
51	52	53	54	55	56	57	58	59	60
61	62	63	64	65	66	67	68	69	70
71	72	73	74	75	76	77	78	79	80
81	82	83	84	85	86	87	88	89	90
91	92	93	94	95	96	97	98	99	100

Example 2

Use place-value patterns to help you **add** and **subtract.**

Find $46 + 50$.
Each row is 10. Start at 46.
Move down 5 rows, or 50.
46, **56, 66, 76, 86, 96.**
So, $46 + 50 = 96$.

Find $96 - 50$.
Each row is 10. Start at 96.
Move up 5 rows, or 50.
96, **86, 76, 66, 56, 46.**
So, $96 - 50 = 46$.

Find the missing numbers in each pattern.

1. 4, 8, 12, 16, _____, _____, _____

2. 5, 10, 15, 20, _____, _____, _____

Use place-value patterns to find these numbers.

3. Ten more than 68 _____

4. 40 less than 63 _____

5. $20 + 50 =$ _____

6. $75 + 13 =$ _____

Number Patterns (continued)

Continue these patterns. Use the hundred chart to help you.

7. 22, 24, 26, ____, ____, ____

8. 41, 43, 45, ____, ____, ____

9. 160, 165, 170, ____, ____, ____

10. 195, 192, 189, ____, ____, ____

11. 33, 43, 53, ____, ____, ____

12. 757, 747, 737, ____, ____, ____

Use place-value patterns to find each sum or difference.

13. Ten more than 30 = ____

14. 3 less than 50 = ____

15. 39 − 10 = ____

16. 68 + 5 = ____

17. Algebra Javier has 74 stamps in his collection. He wants to complete the collection by finding all the missing stamps to make 100. How many more stamps does he need to collect? ____

18. Reasoning On a hundred chart, Tao starts with her finger on 66. She moves back 3 rows and then back 2 spaces. On what number does she land? What number did she subtract? _____

Test Prep Circle the correct letter for the answer.

19. Dan planted rows of flowers. He planted 7 flowers in the first row, 10 flowers in the second row, and 13 flowers in the third row. If this pattern continues, how many flowers will he plant in the fourth row?

   A 14   **B** 16   **C** 15   **D** 10

20. There are five houses on Jenny's street. The numbers on the first four houses are 167, 169, 171, and 173. What is the number on the next house?

   A 174   **B** 172   **C** 175   **D** 170

Name _____

Addition Properties

Example 1

The Commutative (Order) Property says that you can change the order of the addends and the sum will be the same.

2 + 6 = 6 + 2.

2 + 6 = 8   6 + 2 = 8

Example 2

The Associative (Grouping) Property says that you can group addends in any way and the sum will be the same.

(4 + 3) + 1 = 4 + (3 + 1).

(4 + 3) + 1 = 8   4 + (3 + 1) = 8

The parentheses show which numbers to add first.

Example 3

The Identity (Zero) Property of addition says that the sum of any number and 0 is that number.

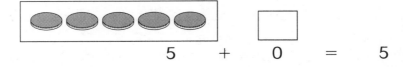

5   +   0   =   5

1. Draw a picture to show that 4 + 6 = 6 + 4.

Addition Properties (continued)

Write the addition sentence.

2. ____ + ____ = ____   **3.** ____ + ____ = ____

4. Write two addition sentences for the picture below. Group the addends in different ways.

_____

_____

Find each sum.

5. $(4 + 6) + 2 =$ ____   **6.** $7 + (1 + 2) =$ ____   **7.** $6 + 9 + 3 =$ ____

8. $7 + 0 =$ ____   **9.** $0 + 13 =$ ____   **10.** $45 + 0 =$ ____

Write each missing number.

11. $4 + 6 = 6 +$ ____   **12.** $7 + 4 =$ ____ $+ 7$ **13.** $6 + 9 = 9 +$ ____

14. Writing in Math Carla ate 2 bananas and 10 raisins. The next day she ate 10 raisins and 2 bananas. Did she eat the same number of pieces of fruit each day? Explain.

_____

_____

Test Prep Circle the correct letter for the answer.

15. $6 + 4 + 3$ is the same as:

    A $6 + 3 + 3$ **B** $4 + 3 + 6$ **C** $3 + 6 + 0$ **D** $4 + 3 + 0$

16. $732 + 0 =$ ____

    A 7,230   **B** 723   **C** 720   **D** 732

Name _____

Relating Addition and Subtraction

Example

Find related addition and subtraction facts that make a fact family.
If you know one fact, you can find the other facts in the fact family.

$9 + 4 = 13$

$13 - 4 = 9$

$4 + 9 = 13$

$13 - 9 = 4$

Related addition and subtraction facts
have the same numbers. They are a
fact family.

$4 + 9 = 13$	$13 - 4 = 9$
$9 + 4 = 13$	$13 - 9 = 4$

Complete the related addition and subtraction facts.

1.

$3 + 7 =$ _____

$10 - 3 =$ _____

2.

$7 + 5 =$ _____

$12 - 5 =$ _____

3. $2 + 9 =$ _____ $11 - 2 =$ _____

$9 + 2 =$ _____ $11 - 9 =$ _____

4. $9 + 6 =$ _____ $15 - 6 =$ _____

$6 + 9 =$ _____ $15 - 9 =$ _____

Relating Addition and Subtraction (continued)

Complete each fact family. Use cubes to help you.

5. $4 + 8 =$ _____ $12 -$ _____ $= 8$ **6.** $5 + 9 =$ _____   _____ $- 5 = 9$

_____ $+ 4 = 12$ _____ $- 8 = 4$ $9 +$ _____ $= 14$ $14 -$ _____ $= 5$

7. $8 + 3 =$ _____ $11 - 8 =$ _____   **8.** $6 +$ _____ $= 13$ $13 -$ _____ $= 7$

$3 +$ _____ $= 11$ _____ $- 3 = 8$ $7 +$ _____ $= 13$ _____ $- 7 = 6$

9. $7 + 8 =$ _____   _____ $- 8 = 7$

$7 +$ _____ $= 15$ $15 - 7 =$ _____

Find each missing number.

10. $5 + 5 =$ _____ $10 -$ _____ $= 5$ **11.** $8 +$ _____ $= 16$ _____ $- 8 = 8$

12. Reasoning John has 14 pencils. He gives some to Sonja.
He has 8 left. How many pencils did he give to Sonja?   _____

13. Write two facts that are related to the subtraction fact in Question 12.

_____

_____

Test Prep Circle the correct letter for the answer.

14. Find the related fact for $7 + 7 = 14$.

   A $7 + 8 = 15$ **B** $15 - 8 = 7$

   C $14 + 7 = 21$ **D** $14 - 7 = 7$

15. Eight frogs were in the pond. Five more frogs joined them. What number
sentence tells what happened?

   A $13 - 8 = 5$ **B** $5 + 8 = 13$

   C $8 + 5 = 13$ **D** $8 + 5 = 12$

Name _____

Mental Math: Break Apart Numbers

Example 1

Find the sum of 26 and 42 by breaking apart the numbers.

Think:

26 = 20 + 6

42 = 40 + 2

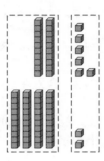

Add the tens.	20 + 40 = 60
Add the ones.	6 + 2 = 8
Put the tens and ones together.	60 + 8 = 68

So, 26 + 42 = 68.

Example 2

Find the sum of 26 + 42 by breaking apart only one number.

Think:

26

42 = 40 + 2

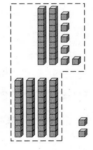

Add 40 to 26.	26 + 40 = 66
Add 2 to 66.	66 + 2 = 68

So, 26 + 42 = 68.

Add using mental math. Use place-value blocks to help you.

1. 64 + 23 = ____   **2.** 26 + 73 = ____

Name _____

Mental Math: Break Apart Numbers (continued)

Find each sum using mental math.

3. 22 + 56 = ____   **4.** 37 + 24 = ____   **5.** 43 + 36 = ____

6. 55 + 32 = ____   **7.** 23 + 21 = ____   **8.** 43 + 44 = ____

9. 44 + 34 = ____   **10.** 52 + 32 = ____   **11.** 45 + 4 = ____

12. 45 + 34 = ____   **13.** 37 + 51 = ____   **14.** 23 + 46 = ____

15. Reasoning Reggie has 25 crayons. Brett gives him 14 more. How many crayons does he have now? ____

16. Reasoning Darla bought 32 stickers on Monday. Two days later she bought 46 more. How many stickers does she have altogether? ____

17. Number Sense To add 24 and 52, Ashley first added 24 and 50. What numbers should she add next? _____

_____

Test Prep Circle the correct letter for the answer.

18. Find 45 + 63.

   A 98   **B** 105   **C** 108   **D** 88

19. Rafael has 47 rocks in his rock collection. His friend gives him 18 more rocks. How many rocks does he have now?

   A 65   **B** 66   **C** 55   **D** 54

Name _____

Estimating Sums

Example

When Amy added 187 and 242, she got a sum of 429. To check that this answer is reasonable, use estimation.

Round 187 and 242 to the nearest hundred to get numbers you can add mentally.

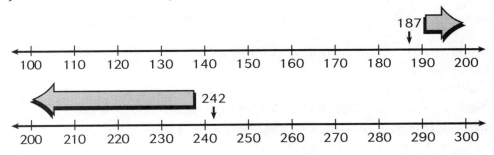

Add the rounded numbers: 187 rounds to 200 and 242 rounds to 200. So, 200 + 200 = 400.

The answer is reasonable because 429 is close to 400.

Estimate by rounding to the nearest ten.

1. 71 + 36   **2.** 24 + 81   **3.** 43 + 91   **4.** 54 + 66

_____   _____   _____   _____

Estimate by rounding to the nearest hundred.

5.   367
  + 141

6.   791
  + 632

7.   506
  + 249

8.   458
  + 891

9. 940 + 190   **10.** 675 + 460   **11.** 531 + 776

_____   _____   _____

12. 369 + 481   **13.** 151 + 260   **14.** 705 + 936

_____   _____   _____

Estimating Sums (continued)

Estimate by rounding to the nearest ten.

15. 68 + 27   **16.** 19 + 93   **17.** 89 + 75   **18.** 54 + 33

_____   _____   _____   _____

Estimate by rounding to the nearest hundred.

19.   819   **20.**   159   **21.** 710 + 678   **22.** 891 + 653
  + 342   + 249

_____   _____

23. Reasoning Jaimee was a member of the school chorus
for 3 years. Todd was a member of the school band for
2 years. The chorus has 43 members and the band has
85 members. About how many members do the two
groups have together?   _____

24. Reasoning What is the largest number that can be added
to 46 so that the sum is 70 when both numbers are
rounded to the nearest ten? Explain.

_____

_____

_____

Test Prep Circle the correct letter for the answer.

25. Which of the following gives an estimate for 79 + 82 when
rounded to the nearest ten?

  A 140   **B** 170   **C** 150   **D** 160

26. Charlie's dad bought a computer that cost $928 and a
printer that cost $254. Rounded to the nearest hundred,
which is the best estimate of the total cost?

  A $1,000   **B** $1,300   **C** $1,200   **D** $1,100

Overestimates and Underestimates

Example 1

An **overestimate** happens when you round up.

There are 183 girls and 198 boys in the school. Each child will get a school sweatshirt. The principal estimated that 400 sweatshirts should be ordered. Will there be enough sweatshirts for all boys and girls in the school?

Use a number line to round 183 and 198 to the nearest hundred to estimate how many total children there are.

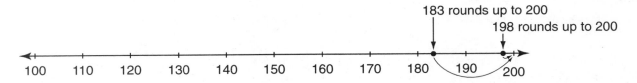

183 rounds up to 200
198 rounds up to 200

$200 + 200 = 400$ There are enough sweatshirts.

Each number was rounded **up** so the estimated sum is *greater than* the sum of the actual number of boys and girls. It is an overestimate.

Example 2

An underestimate happens when you round down.

Jack wants to buy 2 new games. A computer game is $52 and a dart game is $73. He estimated that he would spend $140. Can he buy the games with $140?

Round down to the nearest ten.
    $52 rounds down to $50.
    $73 rounds down to $70.

$50 + $70 = $120 Jack can buy the games with $140.

Each number was rounded down, so the sum of the rounded numbers is *less than* the sum of the cost of the two items. The sum is an underestimate.

Overestimates and Underestimates (continued)

Answer each question and tell if the estimate is an overestimate or underestimate.

1. Use Example 1. If there were 216 girls and 203 boys in the school, would an estimate of 400 sweatshirts be enough? _____

2. Use Example 2. If the games cost $58 and $78, would Jack's estimate of $140 be enough? _____

Estimate each sum by rounding to the nearest ten. Write your estimate. Tell whether your estimate is an overestimate or an underestimate.

3. 26 + 57

estimate ____

_____

4. 72 + 31

estimate ____

_____

Estimate each sum by rounding to the nearest hundred. Write your estimate. Then tell if your estimate is an overestimate or underestimate.

5. 168 + 296

estimate _____

6. 245 + 304

estimate _____

7. 429 + 317

estimate _____

8. 583 + 276

estimate _____

9. Reasoning Mr. King buys 2 bags of fertilizer for his yard. One bag weighs 98 pounds and the other weighs 86 pounds. What is an estimate of the number of pounds he has altogether? _____

Test Prep Circle the correct letter for the answer.

10. Which is the overestimate of 467 + 389 when rounding to the nearest hundred?

A 850 **B** 800 **C** 900 **D** 600

11. Ms. Janey wants to estimate how much money she will need to buy a dress for $44 and shoes for $32. If she rounds the prices to the nearest ten, how much money will she need to buy these items?

A $70 **B** $60 **C** $40 **D** $50

Math Diagnosis and
Intervention System

Name _____

Mental Math: Using Tens to Subtract

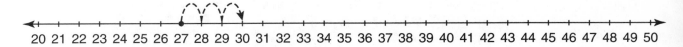

20 21 22 23 24 25 26 27 28 29 30 31 32 33 34 35 36 37 38 39 40 41 42 43 44 45 46 47 48 49 50

Example 1

Find 46 − 27.

Round one number to the nearest ten to make a subtraction problem simpler.

    27 rounds to 30.

30 is 3 more than 27.

Solve the new problem:
    46 − 30 = 16

You must add **3 more** to the difference because you subtracted 3 more than 27.
    16 + 3 = 19

Example 2

Find 46 − 27.

Add the same amount to both numbers to make a subtraction problem simpler.

    27 + **3** = 30
    46 + **3** = 49

Solve the new problem:

    49 − 30 = 19

So, 46 − 27 = 19

Subtract. Make a simpler problem to help.

  1. 57 − 38 = _____   **2.** 32 − 17 = _____   **3.** 61 − 26 = _____

  4. 85 − 29 = _____   **5.** 43 − 28 = _____   **6.** 67 − 42 = _____

Mental Math: Using Tens to Subtract (continued)

Subtract. Use mental math.

7. $32 - 18 =$ _____   **8.** $52 - 46 =$ _____   **9.** $41 - 18 =$ _____

10. $28 - 16 =$ _____   **11.** $55 - 33 =$ _____   **12.** $86 - 23 =$ _____

Find each difference using mental math.

13. $39 - 26 =$ _____   **14.** $57 - 28 =$ _____   **15.** $93 - 34 =$ _____

16. $62 - 47 =$ _____   **17.** $33 - 16 =$ _____   **18.** $84 - 35 =$ _____

19. Writing in Math Round one number to the nearest ten to make it easier
to subtract. Explain what you did to solve the problem.
$56 - 48$

_____

_____

20. Writing in Math Add the same amount to both numbers
to make it easier to subtract. Explain what you did to solve
the problem.
$56 - 48$

_____

_____

21. Algebra Betty has $32. She buys a present for her mother and gets $9
in change. How much money did she spend on the present? _____

Test Prep Circle the correct letter for the answer.

22. There are 53 trees on a farm. 27 are apple trees and the rest are peach
trees. How many peach trees are there?

   A 46   **B** 26   **C** 27   **D** 36

23. Use mental math to solve $57 - 39$.

   A 26   **B** 28   **C** 17   **D** 18

Mental Math Strategies

Example 1

Find $47 - 35$ by breaking apart the numbers in the problem.

$40 - 30 = 10$	Subtract the tens in both numbers.
$7 - 5 = 2$	Subtract the ones in both numbers.
$10 + 2 = 12$	Add the sums of the tens and ones.

So, $47 - 35 = 12$.

Example 2

Find $235 + 197$ by using compensation.

$235 + 200 = 435$	Add 3 to 197 to make 200. 200 is easier to use.
$435 - 3 = 432$	Subtract 3 from the sum to compensate for adding 3.

So, $235 + 197 = 432$.

Add or subtract mentally. Use breaking apart.

1. $54 + 28$ **2.** $88 - 32$ **3.** $67 + 23$ **4.** $75 - 31$

_____   _____   _____   _____

5. $315 + 246$ **6.** $842 + 115$ **7.** $947 - 516$ **8.** $786 - 314$

_____   _____   _____   _____

Add or subtract mentally. Use compensation.

9. $68 + 24$ **10.** $95 - 48$ **11.** $326 + 295$ **12.** $540 - 298$

_____   _____   _____   _____

Mental Math Strategies (continued)

Add or subtract mentally. Use breaking apart.

13. 57 + 22   **14.** 283 + 118   **15.** 79 − 56   **16.** 466 − 325

_____   _____   _____   _____

Add or subtract mentally. Use compensation.

17. 62 + 29   **18.** 35 + 48   **19.** 77 − 28   **20.** 56 − 39

_____   _____   _____   _____

21. 256 + 195   **22.** 618 + 296   **23.** 742 − 394   **24.** 916 − 497

_____   _____   _____   _____

25. On vacation, the Gonzales family traveled 595 miles
in one day. Their destination is 949 miles from their
home. How much farther do they need to travel to
get there?   _____

26. Reasoning Juliana subtracts 39 − 18 mentally by
thinking: "30 − 10 = 20, 9 − 8 = 1, and 20 − 1 = 19.
The answer is 19." What did she do wrong? Explain.

_____

_____

Test Prep Circle the correct letter for the answer.

27. Subtract mentally. Use breaking apart.
697 − 235

   A 822   **B** 862   **C** 462   **D** 422

28. Jenni has walked 65 meters from her car to school and has
to walk another 29 meters to her class. How far does she
walk?

   A 94 meters **B** 84 meters **C** 36 meters **D** 44 meters

Name _____

Adding Two-Digit Numbers

Example

13 children walked to school.
28 children rode the bus to school.
How many children came to school?

① Add the ones. Regroup.

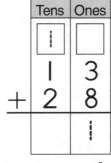

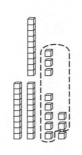

② Add the tens.

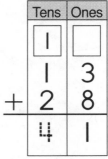

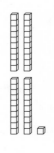

13 + 28 = 41 children

Add. Use tens and ones models if you like.

1.

```
  ¡
  58        56        18        20        46        36
+ 17      + 11      + 19      +28      + 45      +17
  75
```

2.

```
  17        45        32        26        22        33
+ 49      + 14      + 66      + 37      + 65      + 33
```

Adding Two-Digit Numbers (continued)

Anna lost her team hat.
Her number is 44.
Find each sum.
Color Anna's hat green.

3.

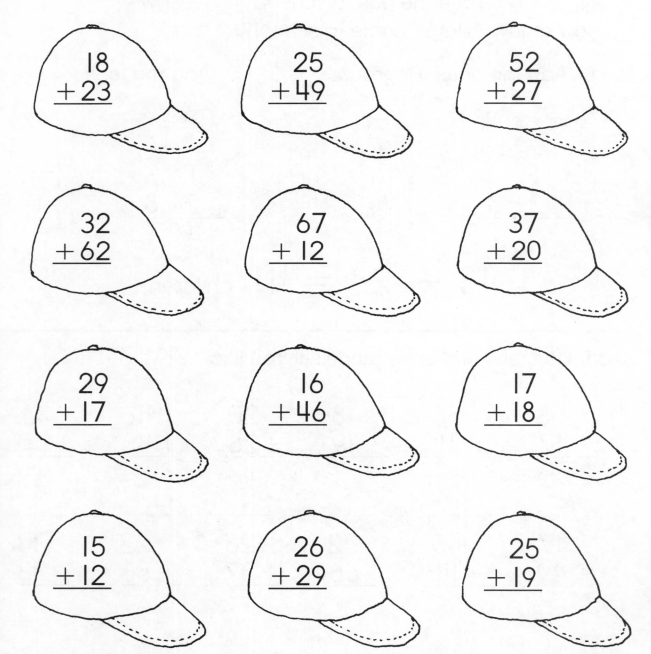

$$18 + 23$$

$$25 + 49$$

$$52 + 27$$

$$32 + 62$$

$$67 + 12$$

$$37 + 20$$

$$29 + 17$$

$$16 + 46$$

$$17 + 18$$

$$15 + 12$$

$$26 + 29$$

$$25 + 19$$

Adding Three-Digit Numbers

Example

The class has 135 books. They got 168 more books.
How many books in all? Follow the steps to add.

① Add the ones.
   Regroup.

② Add the tens.
   Regroup.

③ Add the
   hundreds.

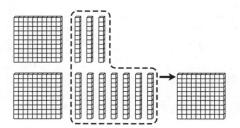
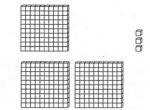

H	T	O
	⌐1⌐	
1	3	5
+1	6	8
		3

H	T	O
⌐1⌐	1	
1	3	5
+1	6	8
	0	3

H	T	O
1	1	
1	3	5
+1	6	8
3	0	3

Add. Draw or use models if you like.

1.

H	T	O
□	□	
1	4	9
+3	7	0

2.

H	T	O
□	□	
	2	3
+3	8	8

Name _____

Adding Three-Digit Numbers (continued)

Find each sum. Regroup if needed.
Draw or use models if you like.

3.

H	T	0
□	1	
1	3	6
+ 2	1	5
3	5	1

Add ones.
Regroup? (yes) no
Add tens.
Regroup? yes (no)
Add hundreds.

4.

H	T	0
□	□	
2	1	7
+ 5	4	8

H	T	0
□	□	
3	5	3
+ 2	7	4

H	T	0
□	□	
7	3	1
+	8	5

H	T	0
□	□	
6	3	6
+ 2	7	1

5.

H	T	0
□	□	
4	0	7
+ 1	7	5

H	T	0
□	□	
5	4	0
+ 3	7	0

H	T	0
□	□	
	8	4
+ 5	5	5

H	T	0
□	□	
8	1	1
+ 1	0	9

Name _____

Estimating Differences

Example 1

Estimate 52 − 18 by rounding to the nearest ten.

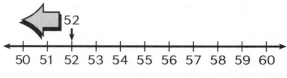

Subtract the rounded numbers mentally.

52	rounds to	50
− 18	rounds to	− 20
		30

52 − 18 is *about* 30.

Example 2

Use front-end estimation to estimate 685 − 279.

Look at the front digit of each number. Use zeros for all the
other digits. Then subtract.

685 ⟶ 600
− 279 ⟶ − 200
400

685 − 279 is *about* 40.

Estimate by rounding to the nearest ten.

1.   47
    − 19

2.   82
    − 34

3. 67 − 51

4. 94 − 48

Estimate by using front-end estimation.

5.   74
    − 62

6.   418
    − 125

7. 81 − 16

8. 945 − 119

Estimating Differences (continued)

Estimate by rounding to the nearest ten.

9.   71   **10.**   65   **11.** 89 − 24   **12.** 51 − 38
    − 12   − 49
                                            _____   _____

Estimate by rounding to the nearest hundred.

13.   586   **14.**   941   **15.** 442 − 181   **16.** 861 − 298
    − 195   − 362
                                            _____   _____

Estimate by using front-end estimation.

17.   68   **18.**   546   **19.** 75 − 39   **20.** 681 − 132
    − 49   − 234
                                            _____   _____

21. Writing in Math The answer to 71 − 59 is 12. Do you
think rounding to the nearest ten, or front-end estimation, is
more accurate for this problem? Explain.

_____

_____

_____

_____

Test Prep Circle the correct letter for the answer.

22. Which is the best estimate for 63 − 24 if you round to the
nearest ten?

    A 50   **B** 20   **C** 30   **D** 40

23. Which is the best estimate for 578 − 299 if front-end
estimation is used?

    A 200   **B** 500   **C** 300   **D** 400

Subtracting With Zero

Example

There are 60 fish in the ocean.
15 swim away.
How many are left?

Tens	Ones
5 ~~6~~	10 ~~0~~
− 1	5
	5

Tens	Ones
5 ~~6~~	10 ~~0~~
− 1	5
4	5

1.

Tens	Ones
9	9
− 3	0

Tens	Ones
8	4
− 6	0

Tens	Ones
7	0
− 1	2

Tens	Ones
4	0
−	7

2.

Tens	Ones
9	0
− 3	8

Tens	Ones
6	3
− 3	0

Tens	Ones
4	7
− 1	0

Tens	Ones
8	6
− 6	6

Subtracting With Zero (continued)

3.

Tens	Ones
7	4
− 3	4

Tens	Ones
6	7
− 2	0

Tens	Ones
4	0
− 2	6

Tens	Ones
6	1
− 4	9

4.

Tens	Ones
4	0
− 2	8

Tens	Ones
5	2
− 2	8

Tens	Ones
9	4
− 5	4

Tens	Ones
7	3
− 5	0

5.

Tens	Ones
7	7
− 3	7

Tens	Ones
5	0
− 2	5

Tens	Ones
6	0
− 3	8

Tens	Ones
7	3
− 6	9

Subtracting Three-Digit Numbers

Example

① Subtract
the ones.
Regroup? No.

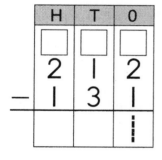

② Subtract
the tens.
Regroup? Yes.

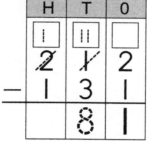

③ Subtract
the hundreds.

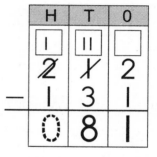

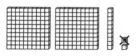

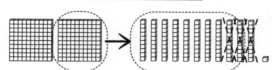

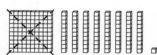

I.

H	T	O
5	2	4
− 1	7	3

2.

H	T	O
6	0	5
− 3	2	1

3.

H	T	O
2	8	6
− 1	1	8

Name _____

Subtracting Three-Digit Numbers (continued)

Subtract.
Use models if you like.

4.

H	T	O
☐	3	18
4	4	8
− 3	1	9
1	2	9

5.

H	T	O
☐	☐	☐
6	6	2
− 4	5	5

6.

H	T	O
☐	☐	☐
3	6	6
−	8	8

7.

H	T	O
☐	☐	☐
9	5	4
− 7	0	5

8.

H	T	O
☐	☐	☐
4	1	0
− 3	6	7

9.

H	T	O
☐	☐	☐
3	1	5
− 2	8	0

10.

H	T	O
☐	☐	☐
1	9	8
− 1	8	9

11.

H	T	O
☐	☐	☐
6	0	4
− 2	9	3

12.

H	T	O
☐	☐	☐
5	2	7
− 3	1	0

Name _____

Math Diagnosis and
Intervention System

Intervention Lesson **F32**

Subtracting Three-Digit Numbers

Example

Find 562 − 378.

To subtract three-digit numbers, you may need to regroup.

Step 1

Ask: Can you subtract 8 ones from 2 ones?
No. You need to regroup 1 ten as 10 ones.

$$\begin{array}{r} {\scriptstyle 5\ 12} \\ 5\cancel{6}\cancel{2} \\ -378 \\ \hline 4 \end{array}$$

Step 2

Ask: Can you subtract 7 tens from 5 tens?
No. You need to regroup 1 hundred into 10 tens.

$$\begin{array}{r} {\scriptstyle 4\ 15\ 12} \\ \cancel{5}\cancel{6}\cancel{2} \\ -378 \\ \hline 84 \end{array}$$

Step 3

Ask: Can you subtract 3 hundreds from 4 hundreds? Yes.

Is your answer correct?

$$\begin{array}{r} {\scriptstyle 4\ 15\ 12} \\ \cancel{5}\cancel{6}\cancel{2} \\ -378 \\ \hline 184 \end{array}$$

Add to check your answer.
184 + 378 = 562
It checks.

1. 439
− 122

2. 567
− 285

3. 856
− 493

4. 337
− 151

5. 165 − 146 = ____

6. 336 − 277 = ____

Name _____

Subtracting Three-Digit Numbers (continued)

7. 436
  − 167

8. 564
  − 285

9. 856
  − 493

10. 337
  − 151

11. 731
  − 256

12. 443
  − 175

13. 561
  − 299

14. 253
  − 167

15. 438 − 244 = _____

16. 826 − 539 = _____

17. **Reasoning** The school has 646 students. One day
177 students left the school to go to an art museum. How
many students remained in school that day?

_____

18. **Number Sense** How many times would you need to
regroup to subtract 316 from 624? Explain.

_____

_____

Test Prep Circle the correct letter for the answer.

19. 753
  − 368

  A 485   **B** 385   **C** 395   **D** 384

20. The school library has 627 books. There are 235 books
checked out to students. How many books are still in the
library?

  A 392   **B** 482   **C** 492   **D** 382

Name _____

Subtracting Across Zeros

Example

Find 6,900 − 1,584.

Step 1
You need more
ones and tens
to subtract.

Step 2
First regroup
9 hundreds as
8 hundreds and
10 tens.

Step 3
Then regroup
10 tens and
0 ones as 9 tens
and 10 ones.

Step 4
Subtract.

```
                    8 10              9              9
                                   8 10 10         8 10 10
  6,900           6,900           6,900           6,900
− 1,584          − 1,584          − 1,584          − 1,584
                                                   5,316
```

Check by estimating. 7,000 − 2,000 = 5,000. Since 5,316 is
close to 5,000, the answer is reasonable.

---

1.   802
       − 561

2.   760
       − 395

3.   400
       − 254

4. $5.00
       − 2.98

5. $8.00
       − 6.51

6.   5,049
       − 2,618

7.   3,605
       − 1,814

8.   9,910
       − 7,865

9.   7,800
       − 4,324

10.   8,050
       − 6,045

11. $50.00
       − 36.50

12. $80.00
       − 29.85

13. $70.00
       − 14.99

14.   6,000
       − 4,560

15.   3,000
       − 1,875

Subtracting Across Zeros (continued)

16.   790
         − 485

17. $24.00
       −   6.50

18.   8,900
       − 1,645

19.   7,090
       − 6,215

20. $6.00
       − 2.49

21. $40.00
       − 25.90

22. $96.00
       − 18.49

23.   3,000
       − 1,480

24.   5,000
       − 2,876

25.   9,000
       − 7,482

26. Mental Math 3,000 − 1,400

_____

27. Mental Math $10.00 − $2.50

_____

28. Algebra What is the missing number?
4,000 − ■ = 3,200

_____

29. Reasoning There are 500 students at an
elementary school. 229 of those students are
involved in sports. How many are not involved
in sports?

_____

30. Jeff bought a new shirt for $25.70. He gave the
cashier $40.00. How much change did he get? _____

Test Prep Circle the correct letter for the answer.

31. What is 3,500 − 1,875?

   A 1,625   **B** 2,375   **C** 4,375   **D** 2,425

32. Tulio took his cat to the vet for shots which cost $15.25. He
paid with a $20 bill. How much change did he get?

   A $5.75   **B** $4.25   **C** $5.25   **D** $4.75

Adding and Subtracting Money

Example

You can buy these blocks.

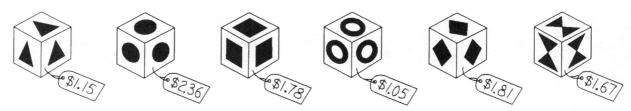

Find the cost for each set of 2 blocks.

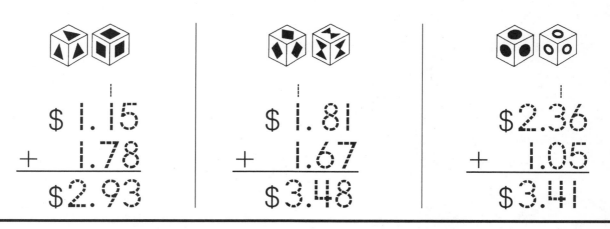

$$\begin{array}{r} \$1.15 \\ +\ 1.78 \\ \hline \$2.93 \end{array} \qquad \begin{array}{r} \$1.81 \\ +\ 1.67 \\ \hline \$3.48 \end{array} \qquad \begin{array}{r} \$2.36 \\ +\ 1.05 \\ \hline \$3.41 \end{array}$$

Find the cost of the two blocks. Then find how much
you have left after you buy them.

1.

You have $6.45.

$$\begin{array}{r} \$ \\ + \\ \hline \$ \end{array} \qquad \begin{array}{r} \$ \\ - \\ \hline \$ \end{array}$$

2.

You have $5.04.

$$\begin{array}{r} \$ \\ + \\ \hline \$ \end{array} \qquad \begin{array}{r} \$ \\ - \\ \hline \$ \end{array}$$

3.

You have $5.17.

$$\begin{array}{r} \$ \\ + \\ \hline \$ \end{array} \qquad \begin{array}{r} \$ \\ - \\ \hline \$ \end{array}$$

Adding and Subtracting Money (continued)

Add.
$1.29 + $2.33

Make sure you put the cents point in your answer.

```
    1
  $ 1.29
+   2.33
  $ 3.62
```

Subtract.
$2.83 − $0.79

```
       7  13
  $ 2.8̶3̶
−   0.79
  $ 2.04
```

Add or subtract.

4.
```
  $ 2.92
+   0.74
```

5.
```
  $ 2.78
+   0.94
```

6.
```
  $ 0.99
+   2.49
```

7.
```
  $ 5.70
−   1.35
```

8.
```
  $ 2.30
+   1.95
```

9.
```
  $ 7.15
−   5.09
```

10.
```
  $ 4.84
−   1.36
```

11.
```
  $ 6.65
+   3.25
```

12.
```
  $ 8.42
−   2.08
```

13.
```
  $ 9.11
+   0.09
```

14.
```
  $ 5.03
+   3.58
```

15.
```
  $ 6.45
−   1.26
```

16.
```
  $ 3.58
+   0.29
```

17.
```
  $ 7.40
−   1.26
```

18.
```
  $ 5.68
+   0.90
```

19.
```
  $ 4.41
−   4.17
```

Choosing a Computation Method

Example

You can add or subtract in different ways.
You can use mental math.

$300 + 100 \rightarrow$ Think $3 + 1 = 4$

So, $300 + 100 = 400$

You can use paper and pencil.

$$\begin{array}{r} \overset{2\;11}{33\!\not1} \\ -\;129 \\ \hline 202 \end{array}$$

You can use models.

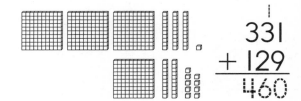

$$\begin{array}{r} \overset{\textstyle 1}{331} \\ +\;129 \\ \hline 460 \end{array}$$

Add or subtract. Choose your own method.

1.
$$\begin{array}{r} 100 \\ +\,700 \\ \hline 800 \end{array} \qquad \begin{array}{r} 600 \\ +\,108 \\ \hline \end{array} \qquad \begin{array}{r} 420 \\ -\,300 \\ \hline \end{array} \qquad \begin{array}{r} 571 \\ -\,326 \\ \hline \end{array}$$

2.
$$\begin{array}{r} \overset{4\;15}{35\!\not5} \\ -\,247 \\ \hline 108 \end{array} \qquad \begin{array}{r} 431 \\ -\,134 \\ \hline \end{array} \qquad \begin{array}{r} 789 \\ +\,123 \\ \hline \end{array} \qquad \begin{array}{r} 624 \\ +\,178 \\ \hline \end{array}$$

3.
$$\begin{array}{r} 167 \\ +\,548 \\ \hline \end{array} \qquad \begin{array}{r} 649 \\ +\,307 \\ \hline \end{array} \qquad \begin{array}{r} 222 \\ -\,74 \\ \hline \end{array} \qquad \begin{array}{r} 882 \\ -\,454 \\ \hline \end{array}$$

Math Diagnosis and
Intervention System

Intervention Lesson **F35**

Choosing a Computation Method (continued)

Think about ways to solve each problem.
Add or subtract. Then write the letter
of the way you used.

A. models   B. pencil and paper   C. mental math

4.
$$643 - 200$$
$$576 + 392$$
$$962 + 24$$
$$234 + 456$$

I used ___ .   I used ___ .   I used ___ .   I used ___ .

5.
$$666 + 166$$
$$100 + 825$$
$$686 - 392$$
$$75 + 170$$

I used ___ .   I used ___ .   I used ___ .   I used ___ .

6.
$$999 - 111$$
$$679 - 402$$
$$794 - 210$$
$$821 - 557$$

I used ___ .   I used ___ .   I used ___ .   I used ___ .

Adding Greater Numbers

Example

Find 23,478 + 17,923.

Add each column. Regroup as necessary.

Step 1 Add the ones.	**Step 2** Add the tens.	**Step 3** Add the hundreds.	**Step 4** Add the thousands.	**Step 5** Add the ten thousands.
$\overset{1}{2}3,47\mathbf{8}$ $+\ 17,923$ $\overline{\qquad 1}$	$\overset{11}{23},4\mathbf{78}$ $+\ 17,923$ $\overline{\qquad 01}$	$\overset{1\ 11}{23},\mathbf{478}$ $+\ 17,923$ $\overline{\quad 401}$	$\overset{11\ 11}{23},\mathbf{478}$ $+\ 17,923$ $\overline{1,401}$	$\overset{11\ 11}{\mathbf{2}3},478$ $+\ 17,923$ $\overline{41,401}$

Check by estimating: 20,000 + 20,000 = 40,000. The answer
is reasonable because 41,401 is close to 40,000.

---

1. 7,169
+ 1,943

2. 4,275
+ 2,786

3. 5,184
+ 2,936

4. 2,943
+ 178

5. $38.64
+ 19.98

6. $475.98
+ 269.23

7. 12,975
+ 8,166

8. 42,973
+ 17,127

9. $245.89
174.03
+ 108.25

10. 71,043
9,481
+ 6,055

11. 5,460 + 18,951 + 23,049

_____

12. 41,500 + 13,957 + 8,955

_____

Adding Greater Numbers (continued)

13. 4,379
+ 2,851

14. 5,612
+ 3,399

15. 6,198
+ 1,946

16. 8,157
+   938

17. 21,871
+ 8,949

18. $29.75
+   8.48

19. $45.16
+ 17.95

20. $618.49
+ 193.76

21. 73,168
+ 18,953

22. 12,958
10,175
+ 8,312

23. 4,181 + 3,927 + 1,365

24. 17,914 + 5,845 + 1,619 + 899

_____

_____

Use the table at right to answer Exercises 25 and 26.

25. What is the total area of Lakes Superior and Erie?

_____

26. What is the total area of Lakes Huron, Michigan and Erie?

_____

Lake	Area
Superior	31,820 square miles
Huron	23,010 square miles
Michigan	22,400 square miles
Erie	9,940 square miles
Ontario	7,520 square miles

Test Prep Circle the correct letter for the answer.

27. Find 19,578 + 8,461 + 3,049.

A 10,978   **B** 21,078   **C** 31,088   **D** 30,988

28. Louisiana has an area of 49,651 square miles. Mississippi has an area of 48,286 square miles. What is their combined area?

A 97,937
square miles

B 87,837
square miles

C 88,937
square miles

D 98,937
square miles

Name _____

Subtracting Greater Numbers

Example

Find 56,739 − 38,941.

Subtract each column. Regroup as necessary.

Step 1 Subtract ones.	**Step 2** Subtract tens.	**Step 3** Subtract hundreds.	**Step 4** Subtract thousands.	**Step 5** Subtract ten thousands.
56,739 − 38,941 **8**	613 56,7̶3̶9 − 38,941 **98**	16 5 6̶13 5̶6̶,7̶3̶9 − 38,941 **798**	1516 4̶5̶ 6̶13 5̶6̶,7̶3̶9 − 38,941 **7**,798	1516 4̶5̶ 6̶13 5̶6̶,7̶3̶9 − 38,941 **1**7,798

Check by adding:
  56,739   17,798
− 38,941   + 38,941
  17,798   56,739

You can also check by estimating: 60,000 − 40,000 = 20,000.
The answer is reasonable because 17,798 is close to 20,000.

---

1.   8,156
  − 5,948

2.   14,951
  − 8,965

3.   25,049
  − 12,651

4.   30,675
  − 21,599

5. $261.05
  − 95.14

6. $745.16
  − 394.29

7. $809.47
  − 152.68

8.   68,714
  − 59,856

9.   20,915
  − 14,876

10.   72,560
  − 43,695

11. 7,510 − 3,295

_____

12. $215.25 − $94.66

_____

13. 60,581 − 12,692

_____

Subtracting Greater Numbers (continued)

14. $7,811$ $-\ 2,766$	**15.** $9,056$ $-\ 4,128$	**16.** $19,819$ $-\ \ 5,921$	**17.** $61,250$ $-\ 29,351$	**18.** $\$719.50$ $-\ \ \ 28.95$

19. $\$621.18$ $-\ \ 452.39$	**20.** $45,812$ $-\ 19,945$	**21.** $90,432$ $-\ \ 7,546$	**22.** $\$615.81$ $-\ \ 229.95$	**23.** $52,506$ $-\ 39,717$

24. $8,152 - 965$

_____

25. $\$209.25 - \$37.99$

_____

26. $83,054 - 39,175$

_____

27. Mental Math Find $1,500 - 499$. _____

28. Mental Math Find $8,000 - 7,999$. _____

29. At its greatest depth, the Atlantic Ocean is
9,219 meters deep, while the Indian Ocean is
7,455 meters deep and the Caribbean Sea is
6,946 meters deep. How much deeper is
the Indian Ocean than the Caribbean Sea? _____

Test Prep Circle the correct letter for the answer.

30. Find $63,125 - 18,368$.

    A 44,757   **B** 45,257   **C** 44,253   **D** 55,243

31. At its greatest depth, the Mediterranean Sea is 4,632 meters
deep while the Gulf of Mexico is 3,787 meters deep. How
much deeper is the Mediterranean Sea?

    A 945 meters   **C** 1,845 meters

    B 845 meters   **D** 1,115 meters

Name _____

Mental Math: Using Compatible Numbers and Compensation

Example 1

Find 13 + 21 + 37.

Look for compatible numbers.

Add these numbers first.

13 + 21 + 37 = 50 + 21

= 71

Example 2

Find 67 + 28.

Use compensation to adjust both numbers.

$$\begin{array}{r} 67 \\ + 28 \end{array}$$

Subtract 2 to adjust.

Add 2 to adjust.

$$\begin{array}{r} 65 \\ + 30 \\ \hline 95 \end{array}$$

Use mental math to find each sum or difference.

1. 15 + 45 + 7

_____

2. 38 + 16 + 12

_____

3. 39 + 38 + 11

_____

4. 58 + 9 + 22

_____

5. 13 + 19 + 41

_____

6. 7 + 23 + 8

_____

7. $\begin{array}{r} 54 \\ + 18 \end{array}$

8. $\begin{array}{r} 29 \\ + 24 \end{array}$

9. $\begin{array}{r} 43 \\ + 51 \end{array}$

10. $\begin{array}{r} 77 \\ - 38 \end{array}$

11. $\begin{array}{r} 53 \\ - 19 \end{array}$

12. $\begin{array}{r} 96 \\ - 89 \end{array}$

13. $\begin{array}{r} 33 \\ + 49 \end{array}$

14. $\begin{array}{r} 18 \\ + 36 \end{array}$

15. $\begin{array}{r} 46 \\ + 9 \end{array}$

16. $\begin{array}{r} 61 \\ - 43 \end{array}$

17. $\begin{array}{r} 92 \\ - 78 \end{array}$

18. $\begin{array}{r} 37 \\ - 29 \end{array}$

Mental Math: Using Compatible Numbers
and Compensation (continued)

Use mental math to find each sum or difference.

19. 17 + 23 + 40 **20.** 46 + 18 + 14 **21.** 27 + 28 + 32

_____ _____ _____

22.　31　**23.**　74　**24.**　44　**25.**　36　**26.**　83　**27.**　76
　　　+ 53　　　　+ 18　　　　+ 37　　　　− 17　　　　− 65　　　　− 29

28. Kara read 23 books in September, 17 in October, and 31 in
November. Use mental math to find how many books she read
in all. _____

29. Algebra 41 + x + 19 = 83. What does x equal? _____

30. Brad and Joe want to buy a new video game for $59. Brad has
$26 and Joe has $14. How much more money do they need? _____

31. Billy earned $42 in week 1, $23 in week 2, $28 in week 3, and
$38 in week 4. How much did he earn in the first three weeks? _____

Test Prep Circle the correct letter for the answer.

32. Chris has 23 compact disks, Bradley has 19, and Stephanie has
31. How many compact disks do they have in all?

　A 50　　　**B** 82　　　**C** 73　　　**D** 70

33. 91 − 36 =

　A 45　　　**B** 55　　　**C** 47　　　**D** 90

Name _____

Estimation Strategies

Example 1

Use rounding to find an estimate.

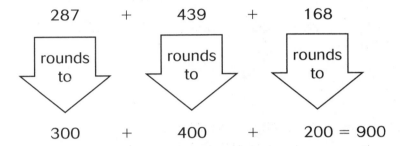

287   +   439   +   168

rounds to   rounds to   rounds to

300   +   400   +   200 = 900

Example 2

Estimate 636 + 159 using front-end estimation.

Add the front digits in each number. $600 + 100 = 700$

Adjust to account for the remaining digits.   36 + 59 is about 100.

636 + 159 is about 800. $700 + 100 = 800$

Estimate each sum or difference by rounding.

1. 57	**2.** 493	**3.** 583	**4.** 4,684	**5.** 1,327
+ 81	+ 125	− 308	+ 2,073	− 958

Estimate each sum or difference by using front-end estimation.
Then adjust to find a closer estimate.

6. 338	**7.** 161	**8.** 382	**9.** 843	**10.** 5,365
+ 427	+ 521	− 168	− 508	− 3,240

Estimate each sum using clustering.

11. 62 + 59 + 58 + 61   **12.** 18 + 21 + 20 + 19 + 22

_____   _____

Name _____

Estimation Strategies (continued)

Estimate each sum or difference by rounding.

13.	39 + 52	14.	218 + 393	15.	967 − 315	16.	6,118 + 2,729	17.	3,040 − 997

Estimate each sum or difference by using front-end estimation.
Then adjust to find a closer estimate.

18.	359 + 134	19.	226 + 558	20.	629 − 443	21.	7,650 − 4,913	22.	8,312 + 1,219

Estimate each sum by using clustering.

23. 50 + 48 + 51   **24.** 69 + 72 + 70 + 71   **25.** 33 + 36 + 35 + 34

_____   _____   _____

26. Morgan delivered 92 newspapers in January, 89 in
February, 88 in March, 90 in April, and 92 in May.
Estimate the total newspapers she delivered in the
first four months.   _____

27. Algebra Ivan wants a new bicycle that costs $129.
He has already saved $61. Estimate the additional
money he will need to save.
$61 + a = $129   Solve for a.   _____

28. Math Reasoning Shayla earns about $50 a week in tips. After
six weeks will she have enough money to buy a $429 television?
Explain.

_____

_____

Test Prep Circle the correct letter for the answer.

29. What is the best estimate for $819 + $288?

   A $1,000   **B** $1,200   **C** $900   **D** $1,100

30. Jerome scored 21 touchdowns in 1997, 19 in 1998, and 22 in 1999.
What is the best estimate for his touchdown in these three years?

   A 60   **B** 50   **C** 65   **D** 70

Name _____

Counting Sets of Coins

Fill in the ○ for the correct answer.

---

1. Carlos has these coins. What is the total value of his coins?

○ 51¢   ○ 76¢

○ 71¢   ○ 81¢

2. Katrina has these coins. What is the total value of her coins?

○ 52¢   ○ 62¢

○ 57¢   ○ 67¢

---

3. Shari has these coins. What is the total value of her coins?

○ 46¢

○ 51¢

○ 56¢

○ 61¢

4. Which set of coins can you use to buy the nuts?

○

○

○

○

Name _____

Making Change

Fill in the ○ for the correct answer.

1. Pedro bought a toy for 46¢. He paid with these coins.
   How much change should he get back?

5¢	4¢	3¢	2¢
○	○	○	○

2. Jo buys a party hat. She pays with 1 quarter and 1 dime. How much change should she get back?

1¢	2¢	3¢	4¢
○	○	○	○

3. Bob buys a toy car for 48¢. He pays with 1 half-dollar.
   How much change should he get back?

1¢	2¢	3¢	4¢
○	○	○	○

4. Steve has 8 dimes. He buys a book for 79¢.
   How much change should he get back?

1¢	3¢	8¢	10¢
○	○	○	○

80

Name _____

Ways to Use Numbers

Circle the correct letter for the answer.

1. How is the number used?

    A locate
    B name
    C count
    D measure

2. How are these numbers used?

Store Directory
TVs and Stereos Floor 1
Clothes - Floor 2
Toys - Floor 3
Housewares - Floor 4

    A locate   **C** name
    B count   **D** measure

3. What number comes before 39th?

    A 38th   **C** 36th
    B 40th   **D** 37th

Use the picture for Questions 4–6.

4. Which toy is second on the shelf?

    A car   **C** truck
    B boat   **D** wagon

5. Which toy comes after the fourth toy?

    A boat   **C** car
    B airplane   **D** truck

6. What place on the shelf is the boat?

    A third   **C** second
    B fifth   **D** first

7. How is this number used?

    A locate
    B name
    C count
    D measure

Name _____

Understanding Three-Digit Numbers

Fill in the ○ for the correct answer.

I. How many hundreds, tens,
and ones are pictured?

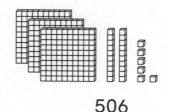

    56   326   506   3,026
   ○   ○   ○   ○

---

2. How many hundreds, tens,
and ones are pictured?

    25   52   205   250
   ○   ○   ○   ○

---

3. Sue bought these stamps. These are some sheets of
100 stamps, some strips of 10 stamps, and some extra
stamps. How many stamps did Sue buy?

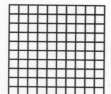 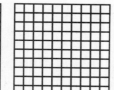 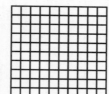 

538 stamps   358 stamps   835 stamps   385 stamps
    ○   ○   ○   ○

---

4. Jodi has 4 bags with 100 beads in each bag. She also has 7 loose
beads. How many beads does she have in all?

   47 beads   114 beads   400 beads   407 beads
    ○   ○   ○   ○

Place-Value Patterns

Circle the correct letter for the answer.

1. **Which is the number in standard form?**

   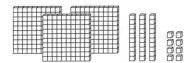

   A 308   C 38

   B 388   D 338

2. **Which is the number in standard form?**

   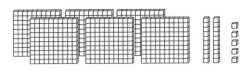

   A 265   C 642

   B 625   D 652

3. **Gloria has four hundred sixty-two marbles. Which is the standard form for this number?**

   A 462   C 46

   B 460   D 624

4. **Julio shows nine hundred forty-six with place-value blocks. What number does he show?**

   A 469   C 649

   B 946   D 94

5. **Which is the expanded form of 577?**

   A 500 + 57

   B 500 + 50 + 7

   C 500 + 70 + 7

   D 700 + 70 + 7

6. **There are 327 people in the movie theater. Which is the word form for the number?**

   A three hundred seventy-two

   B two hundred thirty-seven

   C three hundred thirty-seven

   D three hundred twenty-seven

7. **If you rename hundreds as tens, how many tens are in 644?**

   A 600 tens   C 64 tens

   B 60 tens   D 44 tens

8. **If you rename hundreds as tens, how many tens are in 927?**

   A 27 tens   C 90 tens

   B 97 tens   D 92 tens

9. **Which is the expanded form of 605?**

   A 600 + 50   C 600 + 5

   B 600 + 10 + 5   D 60 + 5

Reading and Writing Four-Digit Numbers

Circle the correct letter for the answer.

1. **What is the value of the 8 in 8,629?**

   A Eight

   B Eighty

   C Eight hundred

   D Eight thousand

2. **Mary Johnson has two thousand, three hundred seventy-four stamps in her collection. Which shows this number?**

   A 23,740   **C** 2,734

   B 23,074   **D** 2,374

3. **Which is the number in standard form?**

   $$6,000 + 900 + 7$$

   A 6,907

   B 69,700

   C 6,000,907

   D 6,900,700

4. **Great white sharks can weigh up to 7,040 pounds. How is 7,040 written in word form?**

   A Seventy-four

   B Seven hundred four

   C Seven thousand, four

   D Seven thousand, forty

5. **On July 4th weekend, the animal park had 9,184 visitors. What words mean 9,184?**

   A Ninety-one thousand, eighty-four

   B Nine thousand, one hundred, eighty-four

   C Nine thousand, eighty-four

   D Nine thousand, eighteen four

6. **Bay City has a population of 8,542. What is the value of the 5 in 8,542?**

   A Five   **C** Five hundred

   B Fifty   **D** Five thousand

7. **Which is the expanded form for the number 3,082?**

   A $3,000 + 800 + 2$

   B $3,000 + 800 + 20$

   C $3,000 + 80 + 2$

   D $300 + 80 + 2$

8. **Which is a 4-digit number with a 6 in the hundreds place and a 3 in the tens place?**

   A 630   **C** 6,533

   B 6,630   **D** 4,603

Extending Place-Value Concepts

Circle the correct letter for the answer.

1. **Which is the standard form for three hundred seventeen thousand, one hundred three?**

   A   370,130

   B   317,130

   C   317,103

   D   300,173

2. **What is the value of the 2 in 258,364?**

   A   20

   B   200

   C   2,000

   D   200,000

3. **Which is the value of the underlined digit in 23$\underline{7}$,097?**

   A   7

   B   70

   C   7,000

   D   70,000

4. **Which is the number in standard form?**

   $$70,000 + 9,000 + 800$$

   A   70,908

   B   79,800

   C   709,800

   D   700,009,800

5. **What is the value of the 5 in the number 152,309?**

   A   5   C   5 thousand

   B   50   D   50 thousand

6. **Which shows the correct way to write 493,805?**

   A   Four thousand ninety-three, eight hundred five

   B   Four hundred thousand ninety-three, eight hundred five

   C   Four hundred ninety-three, eight hundred five

   D   Four hundred ninety-three thousand, eight hundred five

7. **Which is the expanded form for 68,002?**

   A   600,000 + 8,000 + 20

   B   60,000 + 8,000 + 200

   C   60,000 + 8,000 + 2

   D   60,000 + 800 + 2

8. **Which number rounds to 50?**

   A   59   C   44

   B   46   D   38

Comparing and Ordering Numbers

Circle the correct letter for the answer.

1. **Compare 2,001 and 2,010. Choose the correct symbol.**

   A $+$ **C** $<$

   B $>$ **D** $=$

2. **Marie compared the number of students in each grade at her school.**

Emerson School	
Grade	Number of Students
First Grade	95
Second Grade	117
Third Grade	195
Fourth Grade	171

   Which grade had the most students?

   A Fourth Grade
   B Third Grade
   C Second Grade
   D First Grade

3. **Which numbers are in order from least to greatest?**

   A 657, 675, 756
   B 657, 692, 628
   C 657, 635, 691
   D 657, 660, 658

4. **Which of the following is true?**

   A $4,374 > 4,647$
   B $1,355 < 1,453$
   C $569 = 589$
   D $9,019 > 9,119$

5. **Which lists the distances from least to greatest?**

Distances from Jackson to Other Cities	
City	Number of Miles
Clark	270
Leed	237
Piney	230
Kane	273

   A Kane, Clark, Leed, Piney
   B Piney, Leed, Clark, Kane
   C Clark, Kane, Leed, Piney
   D Piney, Leed, Kane, Clark

6. **Which group of numbers is in order from greatest to least?**

   A 2,673; 2,583; 2,516; 2,561
   B 2,561; 2,516; 2,673; 2,583
   C 2,516; 2,561; 2,583; 2,673
   D 2,673; 2,583; 2,561; 2,516

Rounding to the Nearest Ten and Hundred

Circle the correct letter for the answer.

1. **A television costs $354. What is the cost rounded to the nearest ten?**

   A $400   **C** $350

   B $360   **D** $300

2. **A book has 261 pages. What is the number of pages rounded to the nearest hundred?**

   A 200 pages

   B 250 pages

   C 260 pages

   D 300 pages

3. **Naomi has a secret number. To the nearer hundred, it rounds to 300. To the nearer ten, it rounds to 350. Which of these could be Naomi's secret number?**

   A 359   **C** 346

   B 351   **D** 342

4. **Bill is on a trip with his family. So far, they have traveled 462 miles. What is the number of miles rounded to the nearest hundred?**

   A 400 miles   **C** 470 miles

   B 460 miles   **D** 500 miles

5. **Which of the following numbers, when rounded to the nearest hundred, does not round to 400?**

   A 351   **C** 439

   B 398   **D** 451

6.

Television	Cost
12 inch	$99
19 inch	$197
21 inch	$281
27 inch	$329

Jason bought one of the television sets listed in the table. He spent about $200. Which size television set did Jason buy?

   A 12 inch   **C** 21 inch

   B 19 inch   **D** 27 inch

7. **Which is 442 rounded to the nearest ten?**

   A 500   **C** 420

   B 440   **D** 400

Place Value Through Millions

Choose the correct letter for each answer.

1. **Which shows this number in standard form?**

   $80,000,000 + 700,000 + 50,000 + 6,000 + 500 + 3$

   A   87,056,503   C   8,756,503
   B   80,756,503   D   8,750,653

2. **Which is the word name for 8,700,012?**

   A   Eight thousand, seven hundred twelve
   B   Eight million, seven hundred twelve
   C   Eight million, seventy thousand, twelve
   D   Eight million, seven hundred thousand, twelve

3. **Which is the standard form for the number six million, four hundred fifty thousand, eighty-six?**

   A   6,450,860   C   6,045,086
   B   6,450,086   D   6,450,806

4. **What is the value of the 7 in 73,845,302?**

   A   Seventy
   B   Seventy thousand
   C   Seven million
   D   Seventy million

5. **What is the name for this number?**
   4,700,050

   A   Forty-seven thousand, fifty
   B   Forty-seven million, fifty
   C   Four million, seventy thousand, fifty
   D   Four million, seven hundred thousand, fifty

6. **What is the value of the 4 in 224,759,600?**

   A   Four thousand
   B   Forty thousand
   C   Four hundred thousand
   D   Four million

7. **The planet closest to the sun is Mercury. It is about 36,000,000 miles from the sun. What is this distance in short word form?**

   A   3 billion 6 million
   B   36 thousand
   C   36 million
   D   36 billion

8. **What is the value of the digit 6 in the number 526,332,871?**

   A   6 billion
   B   600 thousand
   C   6 hundred thousand
   D   6 million

Name _____

Place-Value Patterns

Circle the correct letter for the answer.

1. How many tens are in 800?

   A 8   **C** 800
   B 80   **D** 40

2. Which is the next number in this pattern?

   14,872   15,872   16,872   ?

   A 13,872   **C** 17,882
   B 14,882   **D** 17,872

3. How many hundreds name 77,000 in a different way?

   A 770   **C** 7,700
   B 77   **D** 38.5

4. Tami's Greenhouse Shop ordered 15,000 hanging basket pots. If they are stacked in groups of 1,000, how many stacks of pots will there be?

   A 15   **C** 1,500
   B 150   **D** 15,000

5. Which is the next number in this pattern?

   2,481   2,471   2,461   ?

   A 2,491   **C** 2,451
   B 2,501   **D** 2,441

6. Dan has 300 books. If he puts 100 books in every bookcase, how many bookcases will he use?

   A 300   **C** 3
   B 30   **D** 15

7. Which is the pattern for the set of numbers listed?

   12,336
   12,346
   12,356
   12,366

   A add 10
   B add 100
   C subtract 10
   D subtract 100

8. Which is the next number in the pattern?

   18,740   18,840   18,940   ?

   A 18,950   **C** 19,000
   B 18,020   **D** 19,040

© Pearson Education, Inc.

Comparing and Ordering Numbers

Circle the correct letter for the answer.

1. **Compare 2,001 and 2,010. Choose the correct symbol.**

   A +   C <

   B >   D =

2. **Marie compared the number of students in each grade at her school.**

Emerson School	
Grade	Number of Students
First Grade	95
Second Grade	117
Third Grade	195
Fourth Grade	171

   Which grade had the most students?

   A Fourth Grade

   B Third Grade

   C Second Grade

   D First Grade

3. **Which numbers are in order from least to greatest?**

   A 657, 675, 756

   B 657, 692, 628

   C 657, 635, 691

   D 657, 660, 658

4. **Which of the following is true?**

   A 4,374 > 4,647

   B 1,355 < 1,453

   C 569 = 589

   D 9,019 > 9,119

5. **Which lists the distances from least to greatest?**

Distances from Jackson to Other Cities	
City	Number of Miles
Clark	270
Leed	237
Piney	230
Kane	273

   A Kane, Clark, Leed, Piney

   B Piney, Leed, Clark, Kane

   C Clark, Kane, Leed, Piney

   D Piney, Leed, Kane, Clark

6. **Which group of numbers is in order from greatest to least?**

   A 2,673; 2,583; 2,516; 2,561

   B 2,561; 2,516; 2,673; 2,583

   C 2,516; 2,561; 2,583; 2,673

   D 2,673; 2,583; 2,561; 2,516

Name _____

Rounding Numbers

Circle the correct letter for the answer.

1. A boat costs $8,699. Rounded to the nearest thousand dollars, how much did the boat cost?

   A $8,000   **C** $8,700

   B $8,600   **D** $9,000

2. The newspaper reported the attendance at the concert to be 364,918. What is the attendance rounded to the nearest ten thousand?

   A 364,900   **C** 360,000

   B 365,000   **D** 400,000

3. Which is 999,300,489 rounded to the nearest hundred thousand?

   A 999,300,000   **C** 999,300,490

   B 999,300,400   **D** 1,000,000,000

4. Widget Mania, Inc., manufactured 2,487,200 trinkets last year. What is the number of trinkets they made rounded to the nearest hundred thousand?

   A 2,500,000   **C** 2,400,000

   B 2,490,000   **D** 2,000,000

5. Which is 25,314 rounded to the nearest ten thousand?

   A 20,000   **C** 26,000

   B 25,000   **D** 30,000

6. The 3-day sale at Rug World resulted in sales of $190,848. What is the sales rounded to the nearest thousand?

   A $191,000   **C** $190,800

   B $190,900   **D** $190,000

7. The company raised $17,517,859 for charity. Rounded to the nearest hundred thousand, how much money was raised?

   A $17,000,000   **C** $17,500,900

   B $17,500,000   **D** $18,000,000

8. Which is 163,219,299 rounded to the nearest ten?

   A 163,220,000   **C** 163,219,290

   B 163,219,300   **D** 160,000,000

Place Value to Billions

Circle the correct letter for the answer.

1. Tyrone read that the profits of a toy company were $12 billion last year. Which of the following shows this number in standard form?

   A $12,000

   B $12,000,000

   C $12,000,000,000

   D $1,200,000,000,000

2. Which is the value of the underlined digit in 45,813,009,004?

   A 5 hundred thousand

   B 50 million

   C 5 hundred million

   D 5 billion

3. Which shows the number two billion, sixteen million, seven thousand written in standard form?

   A 2,160,007

   B 2,106,000,007

   C 2,160,000,007

   D 2,016,007,000

4. Which is the value of the 6 in 2,378,604,117?

   A 6,000,000 **C** 60,000

   B 600,000 **D** 6,000

5. Which is the expanded form for nine billion, six hundred thousand, fifty?

   A 9,000,000,000 + 600,000 + 50

   B 9,000,000,000 + 60,000 + 50

   C 9,000,000,000 + 650,000

   D 9,000,000 + 600,000 + 50

6. Which shows the number five billion, five million, five thousand, fifty written in standard form?

   A 5,050,050,050

   B 5,005,005,050

   C 5,005,050,050

   D 5,050,005,005

7. Which is the value of the 3 in 639,204,986,241?

   A Thirty

   B Thirty thousand

   C Thirty million

   D Thirty billion

8. Which is the value of the 8 in 87,365,002,394?

   A 80,000,000,000

   B 80,000,000

   C 80,000

   D 8,000

Name _____

Comparing and Ordering Numbers

Circle the correct letter for the answer.

1. **Which list shows these numbers ordered from greatest to least?**

   50,500; 55,505; 55,000; 50,000

   A 50,000; 55,000; 50,500; 55,505

   B 50,000; 50,500; 55,000; 55,505

   C 55,505; 50,000; 50,500; 55,000

   D 55,505; 55,000; 50,500; 50,000

2. **The table shows the weights of several aircraft. Which list shows the weights from least to greatest?**

Weights of World's Aircraft	
B121 Monoplane	1,600 lb
Boeing 747	775,000 lb
Boeing B-52H	488,000 lb
Saturn V Rocket	6,526,000 lb
Wright Brothers plane	750 lb

   A 750; 1,600; 488,000; 775,000; 6,526,000

   B 1,600; 750; 488,000; 775,000; 6,526,000

   C 1,600; 488,000; 6,526,000; 750; 750,000

   D 6,526,000; 775,000; 488,000; 1,600; 750

3. **Compare. Choose the correct symbol.**

   16,398,263,056 ● 16,388,263,058

   A +   C <

   B >   D =

4. **Which list shows these numbers ordered from greatest to least?**

   A 7,890,900; 7,809,900; 5,475,700; 4,979,450

   B 7,809,900; 7,890,900; 5,475,700; 4,979,450

   C 4,979,450; 5,475,700; 7,890,900; 7,809,900

   D 4,979,450; 5,475,700; 7,809,900; 7,890,900

5. **Which choice makes the statement true?**

   465,980 > ▨

   A 465,990

   B Four hundred thousand, nine hundred ninety

   C Four million, nine hundred

   D 4,650,980

Name _____

Rounding Numbers

Circle the correct letter for the answer.

1. **Which is 456,783,123 rounded to the nearest hundred million?**

   A   400,000,000   **C**   600,000,000

   B   500,000,000   **D**   550,000,000

2. **Round to the underlined position.**
   23,456

   A   23,000   **C**   23,400

   B   24,000   **D**   23,500

Use the table for Questions 3–4.

Country	Population
USA	284,796,887
Australia	19,546,792
Egypt	70,712,345

Source: CIA Factbook

3. **Which is the population of Australia, rounded to the nearest million?**

   A   19,000,000   **C**   19,500,000

   B   20,000,000   **D**   19,550,000

4. **Which is the population of the USA, rounded to the nearest hundred million?**

   A   284,000,000

   B   200,000,000

   C   300,000,000

   D   270,000,000

5. **Longs Peak, the highest peak in Rocky Mountain National Park, is 14,259 feet high. What is the elevation rounded to the nearest thousand?**

   A   14,000   **C**   15,000

   B   14,200   **D**   15,200

6. **Which number rounds to 45,300 when rounded to the nearest hundred?**

   A   44,300   **C**   45,385

   B   45,329   **D**   45,397

7. **Which is 156,578 rounded to the nearest ten thousand?**

   A   156,000   **C**   150,000

   B   157,000   **D**   160,000

8. **The Colorado River winds 1,450 miles. What is the length of the river rounded to the nearest thousand?**

   A   1,400   **C**   2,000

   B   1,000   **D**   1,500

Place Value

Circle the correct letter for the answer.

1. What is the value of the digit 4 in
    64,871,298?

    A   4,000,000

    B   400,000

    C   40,000

    D   4,000

2. What is the place of the underlined
    digit?

    98,7<u>4</u>3,093

    A   thousand

    B   ten thousand

    C   hundred thousand

    D   ten million

3. What is the value of the underlined
    digit?

    4,5<u>6</u>0,789

    A   600,000,000

    B   600,000

    C   6,000

    D   60,000

4. Which is 435 thousand, 215 in
    standard form?

    A   435,015

    B   435,215

    C   435,000,215

    D   4,350,215

5. What is the value of the digit 2 in
    125,569,431?

    A   200,000,000

    B   20,000

    C   20,000,000

    D   200,000

6. What is the place of the underlined
    digit?

    7<u>8</u>,125,672

    A   thousand

    B   million

    C   billion

    D   trillion

7. What is the value of the underlined
    digit?

    <u>9</u>,125,496

    A   900,000,000

    B   900,000

    C   9,000

    D   9,000,000

8. Which is 35 million, 189 thousand, 3
    in standard form?

    A   35,189,003

    B   35,189,300

    C   35,000,189,003

    D   351,893

Name _____

Math Diagnosis and
Intervention System

Intervention Practice **F18**

Comparing and Ordering Whole Numbers

Circle the correct letter for the answer.

1. Which statement is true?

   A 12,325 < 12,435

   B 81,234 < 80,345

   C 123,234 > 123,243

   D 78,390 > 79,903

2. Order from least to greatest.

   19,390; 191,233; 119,320; 119,230

   A 19,390; 191,233; 119,320; 119,230

   B 191,233; 119,230; 119,320; 19,390

   C 19,390; 119,320; 119,230; 191,233

   D 19,390; 119,230; 119,320; 191,233

3. Which statement is false?

   A 4,309,785 > 4,308,213

   B 1,234,345 < 1,233,980

   C 3,490,580 < 3,491,580

   D 7,890,980 > 7,890,970

4. Which of these numbers makes the number sentence true?

   _____ < 89,345

   A 89,445   C 89,340

   B 90,234   D 89,354

Use the table for Questions 5 and 6.

Mountain	Elevation (feet)
Mt. Alberta	11,876
Mt. Kitchener	11,450
Mt. Columbia	12,303
Mt. Temple	11,350

Source: http://www.statcan.ca/english/
Pgdb/phys03.htm

5. Which of the following mountains has the greatest elevation?

   A Mt. Alberta   C Mt. Kitchener

   B Mt. Temple   D Mt. Columbia

6. Which of the following mountains has the lowest elevation?

   A Mt. Alberta   C Mt. Kitchener

   B Mt. Temple   D Mt. Columbia

7. Which number is the least?

   A 102,358   C 120,358

   B 102,538   D 120,538

8. Which number is the greatest?

   A 75,092   C 75,892

   B 75,792   D 75,092

Name _____

Number Patterns

Circle the correct letter for the answer.

1. Find the missing number in the pattern: 5, 8, 11, 14, _____
   - **A** 14
   - **B** 15
   - **C** 16
   - **D** 17

2. Find the missing number in the pattern: 72, 70, 68, 66, _____
   - **A** 63
   - **B** 64
   - **C** 60
   - **D** 65

3. There are 4 third-grade classrooms. The rooms are numbered 16, 20, and 24. If this pattern continues, what will be the number of the next classroom?
   - **A** 23
   - **B** 25
   - **C** 27
   - **D** 28

4. Ten more than 67 is _____
   - **A** 87
   - **B** 77
   - **C** 76
   - **D** 86

5. 44 + 20 = _____
   - **A** 50
   - **B** 46
   - **C** 64
   - **D** 66

6. Li puts her dolls on shelves in her bedroom. She puts 15 dolls on the first shelf, 12 dolls on the second shelf, and 9 dolls on the third shelf. If this pattern continues, how many dolls will she put on the fifth shelf?
   - **A** 3
   - **B** 4
   - **C** 0
   - **D** 5

7. 100 − 30 = _____
   - **A** 80
   - **B** 60
   - **C** 90
   - **D** 70

8. Malisa is making a necklace by stringing beads. She starts with 3 yellow beads, then adds 8 green beads, and then adds 13 more yellow beads. If she continues the pattern, how many green beads will she add next?
   - **A** 16
   - **B** 18
   - **C** 19
   - **D** 20

9. 142 + 20 = _____
   - **A** 140
   - **B** 144
   - **C** 160
   - **D** 162

Addition Properties

Circle the correct letter for the answer.

1. **Find the missing number.**

   $5 + 3 = 8$

   $3 + 5 =$ _____

   A 5   **C** 0
   B 3   **D** 8

2. **What is the missing number in**

   $6 +$ _____ $+ 3 = 17?$

   A 3   **C** 6
   B 8   **D** 4

3. **John hit 5 home runs in the first
   game. Then he hit 3 more home
   runs in the second game and 2
   more in the third game. How
   many home runs did he hit in all?**

   A 10   **C** 9
   B 11   **D** 8

4. $95 + 0 =$ _____

   A 0   **C** 95
   B 14   **D** 96

5. **Which will give you the same
   answer as $(8 + 5) + 4$?**

   A $(5 + 8) + 3$
   B $8 + (5 + 4)$
   C $(4 + 8) + 0$
   D $(7 + 5) + 4$

6. **Find the missing number in**

   _____ $+ 7 = 7 + 4.$

   A 0   **C** 4
   B 11   **D** 7

7. **Find the missing number.**

   $456 +$ _____ $= 456$

   A 4   **C** 0
   B 6   **D** 5

8. **Kimiko has 4 CDs. Mary gave
   her 3 more CDs, and Don gave
   her 1 more CD. Which shows how
   many CDs she has now?**

   A $(3 + 1) + 4$
   B $(4 + 3) + 3$
   C $(3 + 4) + 0$
   D $(1 + 4) + 5$

Name _____

Relating Addition and Subtraction

Circle the correct letter for the answer.

1. Find the related fact for
   $17 - 8 = 9$.
   - A $9 + 8 = 16$
   - B $9 + 7 = 16$
   - C $8 + 7 = 15$
   - D $8 + 9 = 17$

2. Eleven people are watching a
   soccer game. Six people leave.
   Which number sentence tells
   what happened?
   - A $5 + 6 = 11$
   - B $11 - 5 = 6$
   - C $11 - 6 = 5$
   - D $6 + 5 = 11$

3. Find the missing number.
   _____ $+ 9 = 15$.
   - A 9
   - B 7
   - C 15
   - D 6

4. Find the related fact for
   $6 + 6 = 12$.
   - A $6 + 5 = 11$
   - B $12 - 6 = 6$
   - C $12 - 12 = 6$
   - D $13 - 7 = 6$

5. There were 15 cows in the field.
   Seven cows left the field. Which
   number sentence tells what
   happened?
   - A $15 - 8 = 7$
   - B $7 + 8 = 15$
   - C $8 + 7 = 15$
   - D $15 - 7 = 8$

6. Find the missing number.
   _____ $- 5 = 8$.
   - A 13
   - B 14
   - C 11
   - D 12

7. The sum of two numbers is 10.
   One of the numbers is 3. Which
   number sentence shows this
   problem?
   - A $10 - 3 = 7$
   - B $3 + 8 = 11$
   - C $7 + 3 = 10$
   - D $10 - 7 = 3$

8. Which fact does *not* belong in the
   fact family for $5 + 9 = 14$?
   - A $14 - 9 = 5$
   - B $9 + 5 = 14$
   - C $14 - 7 = 7$
   - D $14 - 5 = 9$

99

Name _____

Mental Math: Break Apart Numbers

Circle the correct letter for the answer.

1. Find the sum using mental math.
   48 + 31

   A 77   C 69
   B 79   D 71

2. Find 62 + 15.

   A 72   C 67
   B 75   D 77

3. Find 45 + 34.

   A 78   C 99
   B 79   D 97

4. Jen's soccer team won 21 games
   last year and 36 games this year.
   How many total games has the
   team won?

   A 56   C 57
   B 26   D 47

5. Find 83 + 42.

   A 125   C 105
   B 95   D 96

6. Find 57 + 35.

   A 83   C 83
   B 82   D 92

7. Nick has 28 chickens on his farm.
   He buys 27 more chickens. How
   many chickens does he have now?

   A 35   C 55
   B 38   D 47

8. Find 46 + 46.

   A 92   C 86
   B 96   D 82

9. Jon has 35 crayons. Jeremy gives
   him 15 more. How many crayons
   does Jon have now?

   A 40   C 50
   B 55   D 60

10. Find 53 + 12.

    A 65   C 72
    B 41   D 45

Estimating Sums

Circle the correct letter for the answer.

1. **Estimate 28 + 53.**

   A 20   **C** 70
   B 60   **D** 80

2. **Tanya's family will visit a national park that is 215 miles away. Then they will go to see Aunt Mel who lives 178 miles from the park. About how many miles will they travel in all?**

   A About 300 miles
   B About 400 miles
   C About 500 miles
   D About 600 miles

3. **Eddie scored 467 points in a board game. His brother scored 339 points. *About* how many points did they score together?**

   A About 200 points
   B About 700 points
   C About 800 points
   D About 900 points

4. **Estimate 97 + 38.**

   A 140   **C** 120
   B 130   **D** 60

5. **Last summer, 390 girls and 414 boys were in the summer soccer league. About how many children were in the summer soccer league?**

   A About 100 children
   B About 500 children
   C About 700 children
   D About 800 children

6. **Estimate 19 + 81.**

   A 90   **C** 110
   B 100   **D** 120

7. **Alan picked apples on three different days. On Friday, he picked 201 apples. On Saturday, he picked 207 apples, and on Sunday, he picked 112. About how many apples did he pick altogether?**

   A About 200 apples
   B About 400 apples
   C About 500 apples
   D About 700 apples

8. **Estimate 580 + 710.**

   A 1,000   **C** 1,300
   B 1,100   **D** 1,400

Name _____

Math Diagnosis and
Intervention System

Intervention Practice **F24**

Overestimates and Underestimates

Circle the correct letter for the answer.

1. Which is the underestimate of 156 + 238 when rounding to the nearest hundred?

  A 900   **C** 600

  B 400   **D** 950

Use the chart to answer Questions 2–4.

ON SALE TODAY			
DVD player	$ 257	Radio	$ 44
Large TV	$ 482	Printer	$ 91
Computer	$ 873	Phone	$ 53

2. Felipa wants to buy the radio and the phone. Which estimate shows the amount of money needed to buy the items?

  A $40 + 50 = $90

  B $45 + $60 = $105

  C $30 + $40 = $70

  D $40 + $60 = $100

3. Mr. Curtis wants to buy the large TV and the DVD player. Which estimate shows the amount of money needed to buy the items?

  A $400 + $200 = $600

  B $500 + $300 = $800

  C $500 + 400 = $900

  D $100 + $300 = $400

4. Terri wants to buy the printer and the phone. Which estimate shows the amount of money needed to buy the items?

  A $40 + $50 = $90

  B $50 + $60 = $110

  C $90 + $50 = $140

  D $30 + $50 = $80

5. Jan needs 126 signs for her school fair. She made 58 one day and 74 the next day. Does she have enough? Which estimate tells how many signs she has made?

  A 50 + 70 = 120

  B 60 + 80 = 140

  C 60 + 70 = 130

  D 70 + 70 = 140

6. A class needs $160 for a trip. At a car wash they made $79 one day and $62 the next day. Which estimate tells if they made enough?

  A $80 + $80 = $160

  B $70 + $60 = $130

  C $80 + $60 = $140

  D $80 + $50 = $130

Mental Math: Using Tens to Subtract

Circle the correct letter for the answer.

1. **Find the difference using mental math. 45 − 28**

   A 27   C 17
   B 16   D 18

2. **Mr. Stone drives 52 miles to see his grandchildren. If he has already driven 37 miles, how many more miles does he have to drive?**

   A 15   C 25
   B 26   D 14

3. **Find the difference using mental math. 84 − 77**

   A 17   C 27
   B 7   D 16

4. **There are 29 people sitting in the theater. It holds 95. How many more people can sit in the theater?**

   A 56   C 66
   B 75   D 76

5. **Find the difference using mental math. 66 − 28**

   A 48   C 27
   B 37   D 38

Use the chart below to answer Questions 6–8. Use mental math to solve.

Magazine Sales	
Grade	Magazines Sold
1	37
2	46
3	61

6. **How many more magazines did the third graders sell than the second graders?**

   A 24   C 25
   B 15   D 14

7. **How many more magazines would the first graders have to sell to equal the number that the second graders sold?**

   A 9   C 19
   B 8   D 11

8. **How many more magazines did the third graders sell than the first graders?**

   A 9   C 15
   B 25   D 24

Name _____

Mental Math Strategies

Circle the correct letter for the answer.

1. **Which of the following is a way to add 83 and 46 mentally?**

   A   Add 80 and 40, then add 3 and 6. Then subtract their sums.

   B   Add 80 and 40, then add 3 and 6. Then add the sums.

   C   Add 80 and 46, then add 13.

   D   Subtract 80 and 40, then add the sum of 3 and 6.

2. **Use breaking apart to find 868 + 248.**

   A   1,006   **C**   1,110

   B   1,106   **D**   1,116

3. **Use compensation to find 64 + 18.**

   A   72   **C**   82

   B   81   **D**   92

4. **On Saturday, 352 tickets were sold. On Sunday, 483 tickets were sold. How many more tickets were sold on Sunday?**

   A   121 tickets   **C**   129 tickets

   B   128 tickets   **D**   131 tickets

5. **Which of the following is a way to subtract 75 − 28 mentally?**

   A   Add 2 to 28 to make 30. Subtract 30 from 75. Add 2 to the difference.

   B   Add 5 to the 75 to make 80. Subtract 20 from 80, then add 8 to the difference.

   C   Subtract 20 from 70, then subtract 5 from 8. Then add the differences.

   D   Subtract 20 from 70, then subtract 5 from 8.

6. **On Friday, 378 adults and 498 children went to the zoo. How many people went to the zoo on Friday?**

   A   120 people   **C**   878 people

   B   876 people   **D**   976 people

7. **Use compensation to find 711 − 99.**

   A   609   **C**   611

   B   610   **D**   612

8. **Use breaking apart to find 48 + 25.**

   A   23   **C**   73

   B   63   **D**   83

Name _____

Adding Two-Digit Numbers

Fill in the ○ for the correct answer.

Add. Regroup if necessary.

1.

Tens	Ones
2	5
+3	3

58   55   61   68
○   ○   ○   ○

2.

Tens	Ones
2	8
+1	4

24   42   34   44
○   ○   ○   ○

3.

Tens	Ones
2	6
+1	7

39   43   47   45
○   ○   ○   ○

4.

Tens	Ones
5	3
+2	8

81   79   77   71
○   ○   ○   ○

5.

Tens	Ones
1	8
+1	5

34   29   33   23
○   ○   ○   ○

6.

Tens	Ones
3	5
+3	7

72   70   77   75
○   ○   ○   ○

Name _____

Adding Three-Digit Numbers

Fill in the ○ for the correct answer.

Add.

1.
```
  H T O
    1 3 6
  + 2 3 5
```

335   364   371   361
○   ○   ○   ○

2.
```
  H T O
    5 4 6
  +   1 1
```

557   567   577   547
○   ○   ○   ○

3.
```
  H T O
    1 8 9
  + 1 4 2
```

331   329   327   321
○   ○   ○   ○

4.
```
  H T O
    5 3 6
  + 2 1 5
```

699   751   747   741
○   ○   ○   ○

5.
```
  H T O
    3 9 6
  + 2 3 7
```

630   633   620   623
○   ○   ○   ○

6.
```
  H T O
    7 1 6
  + 1 3 5
```

851   841   860   861
○   ○   ○   ○

Name _____

Estimating Differences

Circle the correct letter for the answer.

1. A new TV costs $599. Mr. Flint has saved $204. About how much more money does he need for the TV?

   A About $200 more

   B About $300 more

   C About $400 more

   D About $500 more

2. Estimate 93 − 38.

   A 40

   B 50

   C 80

   D 130

3. A rental store has 278 videos. On Monday, 89 videos are rented. About how many videos are now in the store?

   A About 400 videos

   B About 300 videos

   C About 200 videos

   D About 100 videos

4. Estimate 882 − 279.

   A 300

   B 400

   C 500

   D 600

5. The map shows distances between three cities in the United States.

   About how much longer is the distance from Chicago to New York than from Chicago to St. Louis?

   A About 500 miles

   B About 400 miles

   C About 300 miles

   D About 200 miles

6. Estimate 61 − 23.

   A 30   **C** 50

   B 40   **D** 80

7. A dog weighs 67 pounds. A cat weighs 22 pounds. About how much more does the dog weigh?

   A About 50 pounds

   B About 40 pounds

   C About 30 pounds

   D About 20 pounds

8. Estimate 493 − 126.

   A 200   **C** 400

   B 300   **D** 600

Name _____

Subtracting With Zero

Fill in the ○ for the correct answer.

Subtract. Regroup if necessary.

1.

Tens	Ones
4	0
−2	3

12	17	18	15
○	○	○	○

2.

Tens	Ones
6	0
−1	5

26	35	45	47
○	○	○	○

3.

Tens	Ones
4	8
−2	0

28	25	32	38
○	○	○	○

4.

Tens	Ones
3	0
−1	8

10	12	16	22
○	○	○	○

5.

Tens	Ones
8	8
−4	8

48	60	40	50
○	○	○	○

6.

Tens	Ones
4	6
−3	0

14	16	17	19
○	○	○	○

Name _____

Subtracting Three-Digit Numbers

Fill in the ○ for the correct answer.

Subtract.

1.
```
H T O
3 2 5
-1 2 8
```

195   197   199   187
○   ○   ○   ○

2.
```
H T O
4 6 2
-2 3 8
```

234   230   238   224
○   ○   ○   ○

3.
```
H T O
3 6 8
-1 2 9
```

234   239   237   235
○   ○   ○   ○

4.
```
H T O
6 2 1
-2 4 0
```

379   383   381   481
○   ○   ○   ○

5.
```
H T O
6 8 2
-4 2 4
```

258   254   259   257
○   ○   ○   ○

6.
```
H T O
4 2 5
-2 6 2
```

151   155   153   163
○   ○   ○   ○

Subtracting Three-Digit Numbers

Circle the correct letter for the answer.

1. 548
   − 261

   A 387   **C** 287
   B 277   **D** 389

2. **Lynn has a puzzle with 418 pieces. She has used 179 pieces so far. How many more pieces does she have to put in the puzzle?**

   A 149 pieces   **C** 239 pieces
   B 141 pieces   **D** 231 pieces

3. **Which is the best estimate for 842 − 715?**

   A 200   **C** 300
   B 100   **D** 50

4. 933 − 687

   A 346   **C** 256
   B 356   **D** 246

5. 379
   − 185

   A 194   **C** 184
   B 394   **D** 284

Use the table to answer Questions 6–9.

Total Points Scored	
Team 1	442
Team 2	836
Team 3	731
Team 4	518

6. **How many more points did Team 3 score than Team 1?**

   A 289 points   **C** 299 points
   B 399 points   **D** 389 points

7. **How many more points would Team 1 need to score to catch up to Team 2?**

   A 484 points   **C** 494 points
   B 394 points   **D** 384 points

8. **Estimate the point difference between Team 3 and Team 4.**

   A 400 points   **C** 100 points
   B 300 points   **D** 200 points

9. 453
   − 276

   A 183   **C** 177
   B 187   **D** 173

Subtracting Across Zeros

Circle the correct letter for the answer.

1. Carla must read a 200-page book. So far, she has read 182 pages. How many more pages must she read?

   A 18 pages   **C** 118 pages
   B 28 pages   **D** 382 pages

2. The marching band has 104 members. If 37 of the members are drummers, how many members are not drummers?

   A 37 members
   B 67 members
   C 73 members
   D 137 members

3. $8,066 - 4,782 =$

   A 3,084   **C** 4,724
   B 3,284   **D** 12,848

4. Pat is putting together a jigsaw puzzle with 5,000 pieces. If there are 69 pieces remaining, how many pieces did she use?

   A 5,141 pieces
   B 5,069 pieces
   C 5,021 pieces
   D 4,931 pieces

5. Heather buys a cap for $8.72. She gives the clerk $10.00. How much change should Heather receive?

   A $0.28   **C** $1.28
   B $1.18   **D** $2.28

6. $3,030 - 2,690 =$

   A 1,660   **C** 340
   B 1,610   **D** 310

7. Ellen bought a raincoat for $27.00. The next week the same raincoat was on sale for $25.95. How much money would Ellen have saved if she had waited for the sale?

   A $2.00   **C** $1.50
   B $1.75   **D** $1.05

8. Gail buys a pair of sneakers for $42.95. She gives the clerk a $50.00 bill. How much change should Gail get back?

   A $6.05   **C** $7.15
   B $7.05   **D** $8.05

Name _____

Adding and Subtracting Money

Fill in the ○ for the correct answer.

___

Add or subtract.

1.
$$\begin{array}{r} \$3.19 \\ + \ \$2.27 \\ \hline \end{array}$$

$5.43 $5.46 $5.52 $5.56
○   ○   ○   ○

2.
$$\begin{array}{r} \$1.05 \\ + \ \$3.49 \\ \hline \end{array}$$

$4.64 $4.56 $4.54 $4.55
○   ○   ○   ○

3.
$$\begin{array}{r} \$4.75 \\ - \ \$2.44 \\ \hline \end{array}$$

$2.37 $2.29 $2.31 $2.41
○   ○   ○   ○

4.
$$\begin{array}{r} \$5.29 \\ - \ \$4.18 \\ \hline \end{array}$$

$1.09 $1.11 $1.17 $1.21
○   ○   ○   ○

5.
$$\begin{array}{r} \$3.82 \\ + \ \$4.16 \\ \hline \end{array}$$

$7.98 $7.92 $7.88 $7.96
○   ○   ○   ○

6.
$$\begin{array}{r} \$6.35 \\ - \ \$4.29 \\ \hline \end{array}$$

$2.06 $2.04 $2.10 $2.16
○   ○   ○   ○

Choosing a Computation Method

Fill in the ○ for the correct answer.

Add or subtract. Choose your own method.

1.
$$\begin{array}{r} 241 \\ + 195 \\ \hline \end{array}$$

436   438   432   446
○   ○   ○   ○

2.
$$\begin{array}{r} 523 \\ - 328 \\ \hline \end{array}$$

191   195   197   295
○   ○   ○   ○

3.
$$\begin{array}{r} 687 \\ - 292 \\ \hline \end{array}$$

375   395   388   385
○   ○   ○   ○

4.
$$\begin{array}{r} 384 \\ - 176 \\ \hline \end{array}$$

102   112   108   208
○   ○   ○   ○

5.
$$\begin{array}{r} 503 \\ + 249 \\ \hline \end{array}$$

342   752   742   732
○   ○   ○   ○

6.
$$\begin{array}{r} 490 \\ - 163 \\ \hline \end{array}$$

333   327   337   317
○   ○   ○   ○

Adding Greater Numbers

Circle the correct letter for the answer.

1. Jamaica scores 56,009 points on a computer game. Tyler has 45,334 points and Jermaine has 5,899 points. If these players add their points together, how many points will they have?

   A 51,233 points
   B 61,908 points
   C 101,343 points
   D 107,242 points

2. The Blazers soccer team spent $913.47 on uniforms and $352.05 on soccer balls. How much money did the Blazers spend?

   A $561.42   C $1,275.52
   B $1,265.52 D $1,365.52

3. 712 + 3,592 + 13,025 + 4,821 =

   A 11,610   C 21,510
   B 20,610   D 22,150

4. 6,576 + 23,324 =

   A 28,900   C 29,900
   B 29,600   D 30,000

5. The library checked out 3,559 books on Monday and 3,328 books on Tuesday. How many books did the library check out on these two days?

   A 6,887 books C 7,387 books
   B 6,987 books D 7,887 books

6. 16,581 + 3,703 + 25,984 =

   A 45,278   C 46,268
   B 45,268   D 46,368

7. The Cunningham family bought a couch for $753.90, a chair for $159.75, and a set of end tables for $375.25. How much did they spend for all the furniture?

   A $913.65   C $1,288.90
   B $1,188.85 D $1,488.95

8. 6,275 + 8,971 =

   A 14,146   C 14,946
   B 14,246   D 15,246

Name _____

Subtracting Greater Numbers

Circle the correct letter for the answer.

1. **6,789 − 5,324 =**

    A 1,465   **C** 965
    B 1,365   **D** 465

2. **A model airplane kit costs $27.36. A model car kit costs $11.99. How much more does the airplane kit cost?**

    A $5.37   **C** $15.27
    B $14.37   **D** $15.37

3. **78,639**
    − 26,856

    A 50,683   **C** 51,683
    B 50,783   **D** 51,783

4. **A haircut usually costs $12.86 with tax. On Tuesdays, haircuts cost $7.51. How much can Jay save if he has his hair cut on a Tuesday?**

    A $4.35
    B $5.25
    C $5.35
    D $15.35

5. **Thursday night 36,219 people bought tickets to the baseball game. Friday night 63,516 people bought tickets. How many more tickets were sold on Friday night?**

    A 26,997 tickets
    B 27,297 tickets
    C 27,397 tickets
    D 33,303 tickets

6. **5,823**
    − 3,798

    A 1,025   **C** 2,125
    B 2,025   **D** 2,175

7. **Students at Goodman School collected 1,829 cans. Students at Huntley School collected 1,620 cans. How many more cans did students at Goodman collect?**

    A 209 cans   **C** 309 cans
    B 249 cans   **D** 3,499 cans

8. **55,691 − 32,592 =**

    A 22,199   **C** 23,089
    B 23,069   **D** 23,099

Mental Math: Using Compatible Numbers and Compensation

Use mental math to find each sum or difference in Exercises 1–8.
Circle the correct letter for the answer.

1. $1 + 63 + 19 =$

   A 73   **C** 83

   B 82   **D** 84

2. $\begin{array}{r} 46 \\ -\ 39 \end{array}$

   A 8   **C** 7

   B 17   **D** 27

3. Kayla scored 17 points, Melissa scored 23 points, and Tracy scored 15 points. How many points did they score in all?

   A 40 points   **C** 50 points

   B 45 points   **D** 55 points

4. Carlos made 79 bookmarks. Tony made 53 bookmarks. How many more bookmarks did Carlos make?

   A 26 bookmarks

   B 27 bookmarks

   C 36 bookmarks

   D 132 bookmarks

5. This week Marcus bought a CD player for \$88 and a CD for \$16. How much money did he spend?

   A \$94   **C** \$106

   B \$104   **D** \$114

6. $\begin{array}{r} 64 \\ -\ 18 \end{array}$

   A 42   **C** 46

   B 44   **D** 56

7. Tamika had 95 beads. She used 47 of them on a school project. How many beads did she have left?

   A 38 beads   **C** 47 beads

   B 48 beads   **D** 142 beads

8. $\begin{array}{r} 36 \\ +\ 59 \end{array}$

   A 85   **C** 97

   B 95   **D** 105

Estimation Strategies

Circle the correct letter for the answer.

1. Estimate 237 + 678 using rounding.

   A   600

   B   700

   C   800

   D   900

2. Estimate 893 − 246 using front-end estimation. Then adjust.

   A   500

   B   550

   C   600

   D   650

3. Estimate 36 + 40 + 42 using clustering.

   A   110

   B   120

   C   130

   D   140

4. Cory made $16, $14, $15, and $15 mowing lawns. Estimate using clustering how much money Cory made mowing lawns.

   A $40

   B $50

   C $60

   D $70

5. Keesha scored an 89 her first game and a 73 her second game. Use rounding to estimate her total score.

   A   160   C   180

   B   170   D   190

6. Newell had 237 baseball cards in one box and 653 baseball cards in another. Use front-end estimation to estimate, then adjust, to find the total number of baseball cards Newell has.

   A   800 cards   C   890 cards

   B   860 cards   D   900 cards

7. Mr. Davis needs $7,800 to buy a used truck. He has $2,113. Which is an estimate of the difference using rounding?

   A   About $3,000   C   About $5,000

   B   About $4,000   D   About $6,000

8. The airplane pilot recorded that the plane has traveled 591 miles on the trip so far. The total number of miles of the trip is 1,408. Estimate how many miles are left in the trip. Use rounding to the nearest hundred.

   A   700 miles

   B   800 miles

   C   900 miles

   D   1,000 miles